RACE AND SLAVERY IN THE CONTEMPORARY WORLD: AMERICA 2020

Other Books by the Author

A Brief History of Change

The Origin of Awareness

RACE AND SLAVERY IN THE CONTEMPORARY WORLD: AMERICA 2020

Reflections

Patricia Yunghanns

Race and Slavery in the Contemporary World: America 2020
Copyright © 2021 by Patricia Yunghanns
Second Edition

All rights reserved. No part of this publication may be reproduced, distributed, or transmitted in any form or by any means, including photocopying, recording, or other electronic or mechanical methods, without the prior written permission of the author, except in the case of brief quotations embodied in critical reviews and certain other non-commercial uses permitted by copyright law.

Tellwell Talent
www.tellwell.ca

ISBN
978-0-2288-4857-8 (Hardcover)
978-0-2288-4858-5 (Paperback)
978-0-2288-4856-1 (eBook)

*"Each day nature persists in its existence;
it survives as adaptable to both present
change and eventual changes."*

Patricia Yunghanns

Table of Contents

Preface 11

Part I
Reflections on the Value of a Black Woman 15

   INTRODUCTION: PART I 16

   REFLECTIONS 20

Part II
Reflections on When Blacks were Freed from Slavery.................27

   PART II: NOTE FROM THE AUTHOR 28

   REFLECTIONS 30

   CHANGE IN OWNERSHIP OF SLAVES WITH EQUALITY 38

   Equality: America's Founding Definition 44

   CHANGE IN LANDSCAPE FOR SLAVERY WITH VOTE: PUNISHMENT 48

   Punishment for Disobedience..58

   From Punishment to Totalitarianism..60

      Another Frozen Ice Cream Flavor: Vote 68
      Michael Bloomberg 68

   Regime Elevation through Authority 72

   Active Devaluation of Individuals..76

   Alexis de Tocqueville and The American Vote 78

FEROCIOUS DETERMINATION TO ENSLAVE US: Take our Rights .. 84

Obligations versus Rights 86

Attempts by Government to Deprive us of our Right to be Equal to Them 88

Slavery and Obedience 90

    Francis McIntosh: Can McIntosh Own a Part of His Life? 94
    Emmet Till 99
    Rodney King 99
    George Floyd 100
    Breonna Taylor 101
    Deja Stallings 101
    Patricia Yunghanns: Opportunity for Racial Division 102
    To be Overly Fair to Government 111

Who is more Dangerous? 112

    Harassment 113
    Crack Downs 113
    Post Flare-ups of Oppressive Incidents 114
    Impact on Black Women 114

Why Have We Failed to Negotiate Our Freedom? 116

    Our Grooming and Predatory Signs 117
        Strategic Political Warfare: Rights Transfer 118
        Lincoln's intention at time of Proclamation 120
        On Rights, Change, Slavery, and the Need to
        Usurp Individual Rights 121

CHANGE IN DIRECTION OF COMPASS WITH PROTECTION .. 124

    Political Thinking 125
    Enforcement of Punishment: A Definition 127
    Enforcement Infrastructure for Punishment 129
        Degree A 129

- Degree B. 130
- Degree C. 130
- Godlike Character of Political Regime 132
  - Frozen Ice Cream Flavor Coatings 135
  - Division through Enforcement 136

A GOVERNMENT OUT OF CONTROL 140

- Jean-Jacques Rousseau 142
  - Rousseau as a Target of Government 142
  - Rousseau's Description of the Slavery Paradox 142
  - Definition of Slavery on Rousseau's Views 144
  - Analogy of Rousseau's Idea: An Agreement 145
  - The Social Contract: Rousseau's Solution and Active Agreement 146
  - Rousseau's Ideas as Practiced in the Contemporary World: People Participation 147
  - The American Way: The most surprising Historical Change .. 148
  - Rousseau Requirement of Legitimacy for Slavery 149
- Our American Senator: Member of the Political Regime 151
  - Senators need to know the Constitution. 151
  - Senators need to Change their Out-of-Control Attitude. 152
  - Beware of Senators and their Frozen Ice Cream Flavor. 154
- Constitutional Crimes versus Legislative Crimes 155
- Controls Imposed on Government by our Forefathers 1789 157
- Principle Creator and Efficient Perpetrator of Real-life Crimes: Entrapment 159
- Separation of mother and son 160
- Occupation of the Press: Palm Beach Daily News 162
- Formation of a Deeper Parallel State 163

- **CONCLUSION** 165
  - Tyranny and Authoritarianism 168

- **A SUMMARY** 175
- **GLOSSARY** 181
- **BILL OF RIGHTS** 187
- **About the Author** 191
  - Other books by the Author 192

PREFACE

I am sharing these reflections with you because I have been unlawfully wronged and abused. I might say that I have been severely aggrieved by our government. Some might have chosen other ways to protest and voice their grievances, but I have devoted my entire life to quiet intellectual pursuits. So, I have chosen to voice some of my complaints in this book of reflections—in my limited imperfect manner.

These reflections are a part of voicing my grievances or complaints directed towards our government.

My reflections might seem quite legal and historical. That is because I have found that at the root of the problems that I mention, including my own, is law at the mercy of uncontrolled political thinking.

I have included a few words of explanation in an adapted glossary at the back of the book, and it should help with the law-and-history aspects.

Part I

Reflections on the Value of a Black Woman

INTRODUCTION: PART I

INTRODUCTION: PART I

This is a message I wrote and sent to five prominent Blacks. I cannot say that they are aware of my message or that they have read it. I sent this to the following individuals: President Barack Obama, Secretary of State General Colin Powell, Condoleezza Rice, Professor Henry Louis Gates, and Oprah Winfrey.

I sent the message to complain about the fact that:

- the government is overtly breaking the law by disobeying the Laws they are bound to obey.
- one of the laws being broken is Amendment IX of the Bill of Rights.
- my Constitutional rights are being unlawfully violated in 2020, and this affects the value that is placed on every Black woman.

While writing the message, I was somewhat under the shadow of being in awe of the sheer magnitude of government unlawful behavior, the illegal actions of government, and our government's rogue attitude in disrespecting Laws.

In that same cloud, it appears to me that individuals are unable to associate government with committing crimes, even though the government can sometimes behave unlawfully. Our Founding

Fathers' Constitutional Laws are constraints against government, just as government's legislative laws are constraints against us. Our government is simply not above the Law.

Again, since 1789, as we are bound by laws from the government, the government is equally bound by the Laws making up the Constitution, and all government laws are inferior to our Founding Fathers' Constitutional Laws of 1789. Yet, the government has been allowed to break our highest Laws (Constitution) and produce lower laws that are unlawful because those laws merely disobey a Law within the Constitution.

People know that they should not join and participate in unlawfulness. However, when the government breaks the law, most people appear accepting of government's unlawfulness. I can list many famous instances where government has openly broken laws, including their own, and their unlawfulness is publicly accepted and even viewed, as lawful in spite of the obviousness of the unlawfulness.

Is it possible to see or judge unlawful behavior in the political regime, or in documents or actions of the regime, given that the political regime is held in such high esteem? Yes. There was a time when it was not possible to see behavior by government police in terms of lawful or unlawful. Today, there is more objectivity.

Can the government break the law? Yes. Is it legal? No. Is it lawful? No. Should I complain and do so as loudly as possible? Yes. Should you help me magnify the volume on my complaint? Yes.

REFLECTIONS

Subject: Should unlawfulness emanating from our political regime prevail over legal rights guaranteed under the 1789 Constitution?

Four scores and two thousand years after the only ever social contractual Constitution, I stand as an oppressed educated Black woman of color, of the utmost character, who is unlawfully deprived of every iota of the dignity required for being a human. As a Black human and purportedly freed from slavery, I have a legal right to human dignity under Amendment IX of the Constitution.

> **AMENDMENT IX**
>
> The enumeration in the Constitution, of certain rights, shall not be construed to deny or disparage others retained by the people.
>
> **United States of America 1789 (rev. 1992)**

I lay claim to this right that could never have been surrendered, that I do not want to transfer, and that continues to be retained as legally mine. Yet this inalienable right, belonging only to me and owned exclusively by me as a non-slave, has been unlawfully violated in the most audacious of manners.

No one should ever have to turn to Amendment IX of the Bill of Rights because, on one hand, doing so undermines confidence in government and reduces the level of deference and reverence paid to the three branches; on the other hand, Amendment IX was only meant to be a precaution in the event of bad faith demonstrated by unlawful acts emanating from and/or unlawful actions exhibited by any of the three branches.

To overlook Amendment IX is to overlook the strength of history. For history will eventually not be a kind judge of those who select politically feasible unlawful oppression over lawfulness and human value. In effect, to give more credibility and worth to unlawful acts emanating from or perpetrated by any branch over the constitutionally lawful human-valued worth attached to a Black woman of color is wrong.

However, the overarching question that I ask is whether we are still slaves to be considered free only at the usefulness, interest, and convenience of the most ambitious and politically savvy, or are we no longer slaves and are now endowed with the inalienable right of human dignity under Amendment IX, regarding rights we have retained as non-slaves, such as those not capable of being detached from the human in order to have been surrendered?

I say to you, that complacent complicity including conspiring with, collaborating with, cooperating with the unlawful denigration of a Black woman and the unlawful violation of a Black woman's human dignity, teaches the world that Blacks have no value other than that which has been imposed upon us.

I have demonstrated standards well beyond the ordinary, in many areas. Yet I have never been a self-promoter and would rather not become one.

It is expected that I should be considered an anomaly. However, I believe that it is wrong for Blacks to encourage or be complacently complicit about our being defined based on the expectations that have been projected upon us or about attempts to force us to fit false labels or false stereotypes. When the intellectual work of a Black person is not understood, their intellectual work should not be sabotaged to reflect diminished standards, vulgarity, classlessness, and the like; the person should not be deprived of the ability to generate an income, and should not be subjected to other forms of unusual humiliation. The not-understood intellectual work does not automatically mean the Black person is contemplating or has contemplated illegal activities, and it does not mean that the Black person is engaging in or has engaged in illegal activities. It is simply wrong that the type of reasoning that represents the status quo does not describe who we are.

If, in the year of 2020, a Black educated woman of the highest level of character can so easily be oppressed and unlawfully deprived of basic human dignity in the most brazen and conspicuous manner, are we truly more accepted as five-fifths humans than we were in 1789?

Believe me when I say that it is with the deepest sadness that I have turned to each of you, given that you, your family, and any entity connected to you deserve not to have your rights unlawfully violated by unlawful acts emanating from either the legislative, judicial, or executive branch.

Unfortunately, this is not really my personal issue. The necessity of lawfulness and dignity attached to a living entity in order for that entity to be categorized as human rather than a dog and so on, are both issues of every future human that will exist and respire tomorrow, in this country that you and I love so much today.

I am imploring you to overtly and categorically reject UNLAWFUL acts and UNLAWFUL actions. You can do this with support for all my intellectual work: for example, encourage people to subscribe to my Human Rights News channel on YouTube, view my videos especially in respect to Nelson Mandela, and encourage people to read my book, *The Origin of Awareness*. A hardcover copy of *The Origin of Awareness* can be found on this Barnes and Noble page:

https://m.barnesandnoble.com/w/
the-origin-ofawareness-patricia-
yunghanns/1137510350?e an=9781649901583

Again, please do not embrace the UNLAWFUL violation of Amendment IX of the Bill of Rights in our highest Law, the 1789 Constitution.

Part II

Reflections on When Blacks were Freed from Slavery

PART II: NOTE FROM THE AUTHOR

PART II: NOTE FROM THE AUTHOR

I originally wrote these thoughts with the intention of publishing them in the *Amsterdam News* as an advertorial. These reflections might probably appear to cover quite a bit of law and history, but hopefully you will follow through to the end. Helpful terms can be found in the glossary section at the back of this book.

Race and Slavery in the Contemporary World: America 2020

REFLECTIONS

The question of when Blacks were freed from slavery, and the changes that accompanied freedom, are a compelling topic. I can start with the fact that our revolution, which led to the founding of America, was a war of independence from the monarchy sitting in London. When we look at the word monarchy, we find the word "archi" from Greek meaning *leader*, and "mon" from French that means *my*. Monarchy gives "my leader." By revolting against the monarchy, and by prevailing, our revolution rejected leadership as it was practiced at the time.

However, there were disagreements between us because our values and expectations were not in the same place as those of certain ambitious politically trained minds among us, who saw the revolution as an opportunity to free themselves of oversight from London: judicial oversight of the Privy Council, legislative oversight from London's Parliament, and executive oversight from the Crown as a whole. For the ambitious political mind, our values and expectations found in the spirit of the revolution never really registered above their own ambitious interests. So, they would always wait for the right opportunity to exploit the new regime in their favor. Fortunately, in the spirit of the revolution, some insisted that they would only agree to the Constitution if precautionary measures were taken as a backup to ensure individual rights and liberties would always prevail in America. These precautionary measures form the Bill of Rights or the first ten amendments of the Constitution.

Therefore, it is appropriate that I should approach this subject further. Some of the participants during the negotiations of the agreement, for the Constitution, only agreed to the Constitution subject to the inclusion of safeguards to prevent an expansion of powers of the political regime and prevent a diminution or invasion of individual rights and liberties. Since the 1789 Constitution was passed as a result of the American Revolutionary War, that is symbolized by the July 4th, 1776 Declaration of Independence, the founding spirit made obvious that the points of the Bill of Rights were self-evident. It was unambiguous that the political regime would have neither the powers of governments existing at the time in other countries, nor the powers of governments of the past. The American government would become the first genuine political experiment of the Enlightenment period. This meant that powers of the government would be diminished, and individuals would become the originators or givers of all Rights.

Amendments I through X are de facto amendments since they were adopted in 1791, but they are part of the original 1789 Constitution in law because the Constitution was formed only based on their inclusion that forms a part of the spirit of the Constitution. All other Amendments must comply with the revolutionary spirit of the original Constitution to be valid components.

So, the precautionary measures alone prove that the spirit of the revolution that gave birth to America and to the Promise of America is imbedded in rights and liberties for the individual. Rights and liberties for the individual are our core values and our expectations from those employed by us through the process of elections in order to manage our public affairs using the original 1789 Constitution as the lawful legal foundation.

In respect to Blacks, slaves were offered their freedom to fight in the Civil War; there were also reports that the English had earlier offered freedom to slaves if they were to fight against the revolt for independence. In effect, there was a full Proclamation for the emancipation or freedom of slaves issued by Abraham Lincoln in 1862. Lincoln had been elected President because of his support from the Northern states. We can ask whether the proclamation was a political gesture to help the Northern culture take control of the House of Representatives by removing the extra 3/5 vote given to states for each slave (which allowed the South to dominate the North in the House of Representatives), or if they were the words of a man who believed that Blacks should no longer be enslaved.

There were three main changes implemented at the time of the Emancipation of slavery that have been transforming the trajectory of America in respect to the existence of Blacks. These changes were implemented by the elected individuals of Congress in coordination with ideas of the Executive branch. The changes were introduced in laws and incrementally continue to permeate American values and thoughts. These laws are called the Civil War's Reconstruction laws, but I shall refer to them as the Emancipation laws, or Emancipation-era laws. They are Amendment Thirteen, Fourteen, and Fifteen (dated between 1865 and 1877). From this view, the core of the three is Amendment Thirteen, the Emancipation Amendment for the

Abolition of Slavery, and the others are Thirteen's accompanying associates.

The core change relative to the Emancipation laws consisted of the political regime's act affecting slave ownership. With one line, the political regime stated that individuals could no longer be a slave to another, but in a different line, the regime added that only the political regime would be able to enslave an individual.

A second change, from the Emancipation laws, is the establishment of a system that would allow the modernized slavery of post Emancipation to flourish and grow. The trading of the Black man's physical strength changed into the exploitation of unconstitutional acts for continued denigration and oppression of Blacks to benefit the political regime. By 2020, when a Black man ends up in crimes, it is essentially because he has experienced the cardinal moment when he looked into the eyes of his interlocutor and realized that it is impossible to convince anyone that a Black man's soul is not the soul of a criminal, or a criminal in waiting. Rather than build a life of protest against these real expectations of his interlocutor, he accepts to fit into the overwhelming reality where he has been placed.

A third change from the Emancipation laws was an audaciously condescending transformation of one hundred and eighty degrees in the direction of our country's guiding compass: from individual rights and liberties toward the direction of authoritarianism benefiting the political regime and its participants.

So, let us look at whether Blacks were ever freed from slavery or whether Emancipation was a fallacious ending to slavery with the principle changes I mentioned: our masters or owners; the landscape or manner of enslavement; and the direction of the political regime's compass.

CHANGE IN OWNERSHIP OF SLAVES WITH EQUALITY

CHANGE IN OWNERSHIP OF SLAVES WITH EQUALITY

The first consequential change relative to the Emancipation era laws consisted of the political regime's act affecting slave ownership, or who would be our masters and owners.

As per Amendment XIII, individuals would no longer be able to own slaves. Thus, slaves could no longer be the property of a private individual. This is expressed in the words of Amendment XIII that "Neither slavery nor involuntary servitude… shall exist within the United States." However, Amendment XIII officially recognized and gifted slave ownership to the political regime because XIII follows up by stating expressly the following: "except as a punishment for crimes." The follow up statement invalidates the previous abolition of slavery statement because the "except" statement explicitly informs that all slavery is abolished but slavery will exist as submission to obligations or duties the political regime determines by its own laws. This means that slavery was abolished on plantations but would exist as punishment under the regime. So, the regime became the official master of this non-plantation type of slavery. We know this from the words, "for crimes," that are stated in Thirteen. Just as cotton picking was the domain of the Southern farmer, punishments for crimes are in the domain of the political regime. Therefore, XIII laid the foundation for a change in master or owner of the emancipated Black man.

To put this into procedural context, slaves could only be the property of the regime and subject to content and procedural decisions made by the political regime.

Rather than a non-slave purchasing a slave, the political regime could formalize its own ideas into law that engender ownership rights over individuals. Thus, XIII officially changed the owner or master of slavery from the private individual property owner to the political regime.

So, when the ink dried and night fell on December 6, 1865, the day the XIII Amendment was adopted, we were still marked for slavery, and we were still not officially declared 5/5 fully human. So, XIII did not emancipate us. It changed our master. This will become more obvious when we consider the second major change of the Emancipation laws.

How would this change play out in society politically? The political regime accompanied its official slave owning status with the frozen ice cream coating concept of equality distributed to individuals in respect to its laws and cited the word, "equal" in Amendment XIV of the Emancipationera laws. However, any mention of equality subsequent to Amendment XIII can be viewed as disingenuous because Amendment XIII marked all men for slavery under the regime. Why would Blacks seek equality of all slaves?

Note on Conflict from the Transfer of Ownership of the Slave

> Under the old slavery system, the slave was worth a certain price. That price was considered assets of or financial value of the master. The slave owner was sometimes willing to sell the slave to a new owner at that given price; the slave could also pay that price and purchase ownership of himself. However, if a slave ran away, the owner lost the price of the slave; therefore, a runaway slave was considered a thief who'd stolen the price, at which he was valued, from the slave master's bank account.
>
> With Emancipation, something legal changed and something political changed.
>
> - From a legal standpoint, there was a transfer of ownership. When the slaves were freed, the ownership of the slaves was passed from the plantation owner to the slaves (at least, in appearance). The old masters were at a loss: the abolition of slavery meant that each slave took their own value from the former master's bank account. The slave "stole" from the White slave owner or was given property (ownership of himself) belonging to the White slave owner for nothing.

- From a political standpoint, while the political regime was praised for giving Blacks ownership of themselves (freeing the Blacks), in fact the regime passed legal ownership from the old masters to themselves (to the regime). The Blacks carried the blame for receiving ownership, and the regime knowingly not only allowed them to take the blame for getting ownership, it did so without compensating the former owners, even though the Constitution specifically does not allow government to remove property without compensating. (See the example of the brothers and the toy.) The regime directly profited from Emancipation, now possessing the rights of freed Blacks. These rights allowed for authority or prestige, deference, reverence, etc...The regime became the "master forever" because it now could control, give, and adjust the rights of all Blacks.

Equality: America's Founding Definition

When used by our Founding Fathers and in relationship to our Constitution, *equal* or *equality* meant "equal to the king who is our leader." This is an extraordinary and extremely revolutionary idea for its time.

It meant that the king is not worth more than us, or the king is not above each individual. Each of us, just like the king, was born as humans. We were born equal and that equality is in each of our "intrinsic and unalienable" rights and liberties. So, the king (our leader), who is our equal because he is a human, cannot control or own our rights and liberties. It was to be so basic that it was not really to require further explanation. They used the words *self-evident* to describe this equality.

However, as the political regime freed Blacks, they directed us toward a new form of equality—the form that Alexis de Tocqueville appreciated, and the same equality that led to the 1804 dictatorship of Napoleon in France. This definition of equality makes each individual the police of every other individual because each one needs an equality measuring tool that must be checked. It also elevates the authority of the political regime because the political thinking automatically seizes the role of arbiter and referee who will make sure that this equality exists and that no one tries to cheat.

In effect, this French version of equality that I just described is equality between each other, but the American equality that created our Constitution is equality between each individual and our leadership (the king). Blacks were entitled to the hypocrisy of equality enjoyed by Whites when Alexis de Tocqueville visited America. (See p. [insert page] for more information about de Tocqueville.)

Freeing Blacks should have meant presenting a path to a life for rights and liberties rather than a road to equality under the political regime's equal enslavement strategic idea.

CHANGE IN LANDSCAPE FOR SLAVERY WITH VOTE: PUNISHMENT

As I mentioned, the core change relative to the Emancipation laws consisted of the political regime's act affecting slave ownership. With one line, the political regime stated that individuals could no longer be a slave to another, but in a different line, the regime added that only the political regime would be able to enslave an individual. As the participants of the political regime freed the Black man from plantation chains, they simultaneously installed the foundation for the Black man's eventual prison chains.

A new foundation laid for post-Emancipation enslavement of Blacks constitutes the second sweeping change emanating from the Emancipation laws. The trading of financially purchased physical labor of the Black man, changed into the exploitation of unconstitutional acts for the continued devaluation and oppression of Blacks to the benefit of the political regime. Rather than a country populated with cotton trees, America continues to change into a landscape of unconstitutional acts and unlawful regime authoritarian activities.

In other words, when we were owned by individuals, the symbolic landscape of our abuse was the plantation and the symbolic tool of our abuse was our physical strength or ability in order to enhance productivity of the work our masters wanted done. For the agricultural products, the owners generated money by dealing and trading with other traders and businesspeople. With the Emancipation change, the symbolic landscape would become the prisoner's chain and the tool is the unconstitutional acts used to create crimes.

With this second Emancipation change, our abuse became punishment for disobeying the political regime while the participants of the political regime received benefits such as increase of status, wealth, fame, and legacy that befit only a king. Under the pre-Emancipation system, the ultimate profit was money for the individual slave owner rather than direct enhancement of his overall life; the new system allows expansion of power, establishment of historical legacies, and increase in wealth for the political regime participants.

I mentioned that the principle Emancipation amendment number thirteen informs us that slavery is abolished, "except as a punishment." Punishment is a form of oppression, when not related to traditional justice. For outside of traditional justice, punishment is the price one pays for refusal to submit to oppression. It is an instrument that can legitimize any degree of oppression and give credibility to any type of oppressor, under certain conditions.

During plantation slavery or the pre-Emancipation period, our abuse for disobeying the master could provoke a whipping or a sale. Under the political regime, or post-Emancipation, a conceived notion that there could be a refusal or potential refusal to obey our new masters, or submit to their whims, leads to denigration, degradation, and complete destruction of one's self, one's family, and all that might be associated with the disobedient individual.

The new masters' preferred method of flogging is our financial ruin along with our psychological humiliation and denigration instead of a physical whip. By the year 2020, with the political regime as our master, any Black man, along with any human, and any other entity associated with the Black man who refuses to submit to oppression, is vilified, denigrated, or destroyed in any manner available while observers are forced to remain just as silent and accepting as they were during slavery for our labor.

Again, rather than the physical exploitation of our labor, our exploitation changed to punishment if we disobey any acts created by the regime that represents the regime's wishes or ideas. Emancipation's Amendment Thirteen specifically makes a distinction between slavery and slavery in the form of labor when it refers to, "Neither slavery nor involuntary servitude." The new system for slavery of Blacks would maintain the Black man to a place of servitude. Following the newly instituted pattern, if one day, they gave us the gift of equal opportunities to wealth, in the same day, they would take control of all aspects of the financial lives of every individual and create acts to ensure financial oppression using punishment. In fact, the Emancipation-era amendments appear to be constructed to keep the Black man subjected to continued and perpetual servitude.

One way of envisioning the new era of our enslavement based on punishment is through the word "obligation." In this sense, punishment is an obligation to submit to oppression by an oppressor or master who has gained the status of legitimate authority to inflict that type of oppression. So, punishment is tied to an obligation owed to the master. Having an obligation is the opposite of having rights. Obligation means the absence of rights, except if rights are given by the master with legitimate authority. However, America is an exception to this because the political authority who attempts to give rights must also have received those rights as power under our 1789 Constitution in order to be able to distribute them. Since 1789 in America, government no longer has a reservoir of rights they can distribute.

From this perspective of obligation, punishment is an obligation to submit to exploitation, oppression, or slavery at the hands of the person who has a power to inflict the punishment. Since punishment is the obligation to submit to oppression, since oppression is a trait of slavery, and since lack of rights is a property of slavery, the ultimate conclusion of punishment will always be deprivation of rights and liberties. However, under the spirit or expectations of the 1789 Constitution, rights and liberties are property of the fully one hundred percent human individual. The Emancipation's slavery based on punishment was not only attached to obligation but also to discipline because punishment is a manner of instilling discipline by taming the individual through punishment. Punishment tames or trains the individual to correct all disobedience, but the soft political goal is to generate the individual who calls himself responsible toward all regime orders because this would be an acceptance of the obligation to obey the regime and proof of total surrender to all future orders.

In effect, obligation and discipline are not the only words attached to the punishment that would become the new life of Blacks from the Emancipation's reconstruction of slavery. Punishment is incomplete without a rational excuse based on supremacy in order to justify inflicting the given punishment, especially in the form of cruelty or unusual forms that might be contrary to common taste.

So, once the participants of the political regime decided that the new landscape for enslaving Blacks was punishment, they needed a license they could use to legitimize the new form of enslavement of Blacks. The distribution of punishment such as abuse, cruelty, mistreatment, obvious oppression, vilification, and humiliation require legitimacy at an authoritative level. It needed firm authority as support.

CHANGE IN LANDSCAPE FOR SLAVERY WITH VOTE: PUNISHMENT

In Amendment XIII of the Emancipation-era laws, the regime sets out the new path to slavery as punishment that would be inflicted, "for crimes." The word "crimes" is not qualified in this change the political regime added to the 1789 Constitution. However, from my observations of the country, it is obvious to all of us that the word "crimes" refers to disobedience of ideas as policy decisions belonging to the political regime. These ideas are presented in various forms of acts that rely on both content and procedures. The variety of forms emanating from the three branches of the political regime, to which we would be subjected, is a collection of ideas as rules that could be called law (although technically the word "law" is considered as being associated with legislative powers), but there are other names, such as legislation, executive order, regulation, precedent, orders, and the like. The central qualifier is that it must come from one of the three branches (legislative, executive, or judicial) of the political regime.

If the Black man were to disobey one of the regime's many created orders, the Black commits an infraction, or a type of sin, against the orders of one of the branches of the political regime. The regime can refer to this sin, by the word crime, as in

Emancipation Amendment XIII. Since punishment needs this element of authority or supremacy in order to not be referred to as barbaric and other like words, the political regime would eventually create and elevate their existence to the highest level of authority. Their ideas of policy in form of laws would act as justification and elevators of their position as slave owner and master, as well as for authority or superiority.

Punishment for Disobedience

However, the only possible way for crimes to ever exist is if the regime labels an event a crime and redacts the event into regime content and regime procedures. In other words, the political regime must create an order to be disobeyed such that a crime can exist. Once the regime has created a law-based crime to which the regime has attached a punishment, only then can the Black man be punished for disobeying the regime. Again, a crime must be created by the regime and the regime must attach a punishment to the crime for the Black man to be recruited as a slave. This, of course, could be extended to the fear in society of constantly working hard to ensure that the regime is being obeyed. In other words, the landscape change for slavery became punishment for disobeying the regime. So, for the post Emancipation Black man, he would carry out his life not only in chains, but burdened with psychological fear of disobeying his master and being vilified.

From Punishment to Totalitarianism

With the creation of a new slavery landscape of punishment for disobedience and while the Black man lived in fear of punishment, the political regime would build their material legacy and their historical legacy using their political thinking.

I attach five components to the process of political thinking: having been encouraged to like benefits; learned to spot beneficial opportunities; learned to exploit opportunities for benefits; learned to groom targets; and learned to reinvent justifications, such as pass the blame.

Since strategic exploitation of opportunities for a benefit is a property of the political thinking process, one should not expect the participants of the political regime to be capable of caring about Blacks unless they have calculated an obtainable benefit. Benefit refers to serving their interest, being convenient for them, or some type of profit. The political thinking default will be a drive to exploit and dominate.

However, the 1789 Constitution severely limited the political regime's power. It also transferred the notion of originator or giver of rights from the regime to each individual. Although there are countries that have transferred the giver of rights status to the people of the country as a group represented often in the verbal symbol, "We the People," with a capital P, no other country had ever transferred originating rights to individuals, and no other country has ever transferred originating rights to individuals. America remains the only country to have done so with the 1789 Constitution. This means that the 1789 Constitution reduced the regime participants from leaders or from the Greek "archi" to employees.

The founding Constitution removed the power to distribute rights from the political regime, in spite of scholarly enumerated rights. In other words, the political regime, including Congress, has no power to give any rights whatsoever since 1789 because, in 1789, rights became property of nonslaves or of one hundred percent full humans. This means that the Bill of Rights are obligations to which the political regime is required to submit. In effect, the amendments of the Bill of Rights were precautionary measures that represent rights that had never been surrendered, but were also rights that any politically savvy mind would sooner or later be driven to control. They are listed to be used only in the event the regime pursued an antiindividual rights and liberties path. I might also add that only some rights were delegated to the regime for the purpose of fulfilling the powers in the Constitution, but that fulfilment cannot lawfully be expanded beyond the rights that were initially given up without a new constitution.

In effect, the limitations of the political regime's power pursuant to the 1789 Constitution and its spirit or expectations, are extraordinarily severe. They are the severest in the world. Once more, the political regime's participants became employees rather than leaders in the traditional sense. They would be hired mainly through the process of elections to pave, manage, and develop the public affairs of the newly formed United States of America, along a new path forward on the principle of individual rights and liberties. In other words, their policies were limited to constructing a country based on the founding principle or spirit of individual rights and liberties.

The 1789 Constitution also indicated that it no longer saw punishment as a positive under the new system of individual rights and liberties. This is expressed in Article VIII of the Bill of Rights where we learn that the political regime had not been given the power to inflict cruel and unusual punishment. This is not an attack on laws that create punishment. Laws are good, useful, and a means for obtaining justice. However, they can also become a special tool in the hands of the political savvy.

Since 1789, the strategic ideas or policy content of the political regime are no longer lawful merely because they are formed in content as law and respect all procedural necessities. They now also need to obey the highest law, the Constitution of 1789. To help ensure the obedience and adherence to the Constitution as well as curtail the political drive, a system of checks and balances was instituted along with the concept of separation of powers. Each has been reduced over the years to a mostly non-operating system.

In spite of this failure, the lawful position still stands. Again, the political regime no longer has lawful power to create all the laws needed to change their policy ideas into law; the political regime no longer has power to create all the agencies needed for policing all the crimes the political regime's participants can create. They are now employees rather than traditional leaders; they are no longer givers of rights. Yet, rather than develop and foment America's founding principle of rights and liberties for all, including Blacks, the political regime made itself the epicenter of our public affairs with the Emancipation laws, in the same manner kings and emperors had done in the past.

With the change from our plantation labor submission to our submission to punishment from the political regime, the Emancipation era provided the opportunity for the political regime to direct their thoughts away from managing our public affairs on the principle of individual rights and liberties. The regime participants seized the opportunity to construct a regime just like the other world regimes that were all directed along an authoritarian path. In addition, the new authoritarian path would benefit the regime participants by maximizing their power, wealth, fame, and legacy.

The participants of the political regime would benefit by adopting the authoritarian path of other countries and avoiding a life as mere employees or servants to the people. They would name the ideas of their policies that they put into law, mostly, in their own memory and after themselves. Streets and even entire counties would carry their names. Their State funerals are paid for by the country rather than by themselves. Flags are raised in reverence to them. They are provided with paid assistances, and sometimes money is spent building shrines, in the form of monuments, to support their legacy.

Take this as an example: While Americans were earning less than thirty-five dollars for a hard week of full-time labor in 1922, the political regime spent about three million dollars building a monument to honor President Lincoln, who was one of their own. For their State funerals, they require fuel for at least a 747 type of plane that needs close to 50,000 gallons of fuel for each full tank times the price of fuel. Then we must take into account the body being picked up by plane and returned by plane.

Today, while over seventeen percent of Americans earn less than 26,000 dollars each year, those sitting in Congress (House of Representatives and Senate) earn over 170,000 each year plus extras. We pay to provide them with an Office of the Attending Physician, just in case there are medical emergencies. The average base alone for a Senators' Official Personnel and Office Expense Account (SOPOEA) is around three and a half million dollars, without adding in the extra monies available. While our political regime and its members use their policy ideas as rules in the form of laws to degrade us, discredit us, and humiliate us, they use the added authority and deference they gain to make millions of dollars for speeches and books. Without the added legitimacy to their legacy from elevating their authority at our expense, they would not be making those millions and millions of dollars. For a speech from you and a book from you would be equal in value to a speech and book from each of them. All these elements support the elevation, deference, and reverence of the regime participants.

From the process of political thinking, it also makes the point that whatever the freed Black would have in his pocket is by the mercy and goodness of the political regime that allows him to keep that portion earned from his labor as an individual now freed from slavery. This, of course, helps to build the reputation of Amendment XIII without any intention of ever allowing the Black man to enjoy the rights and freedoms envisioned by the Constitution. It appears that the political regime had no intention to ever become employees of the freed Black man.

Another Frozen Ice Cream Flavor: Vote

Some would argue that those laws also gave the right to vote. However, those laws also put a condition on the gift of a right to vote. The freed Black man would forever only be allowed to vote if he is obedient and obeys the political regime. Disobedience of the regime results in no right to vote. The Emancipation-era Amendment Fourteen specifies that the freed Black can have the right to vote "except for... crime." In other words, he can have the right to vote as long as he obeys the regime. Since crimes are the results of policy ideas from the regime in the form of laws, the crime that impedes the right to vote is whatever idea the regime decides upon.

Michael Bloomberg

To illustrate the political thinking involved in this gift in the form of rights, I have selected the story of Michael Bloomberg. In brief, Bloomberg is a businessman and philanthropist out of New York. In 2018, the people of the state of Florida voted for an amendment (change) to the state Constitution that would allow Floridians with felony convictions (having been imprisoned), with a few exceptions, and who had fulfilled the conditions of their sentencing to be able to vote again without any type of approval from the state. The state of Florida passed a law requiring that felons with any outstanding legal financial obligations, including fines, fees, and restitution, fulfill these obligations before they could be allowed to vote. In September 2020, a charity organization announced that they had raised funds to pay the charges for them. It was reported that Michael Bloomberg had pledged donations of some $16 million to help ensure that they would be eligible to vote in the November presidential elections.

If the right to vote purportedly given by the political regime were a gift, any intervention by Michael Bloomberg to help perfect the gift would surely have been welcomed. After all, if monies must be paid to perfect the gift, would it not be better for someone to pay? The state of Florida responded with a criminal investigation into Bloomberg. Take note that I used the word investigation. I use this word, investigation, later when talking about our regime's journey toward oppression rather than toward America's founding principle of individual rights and liberties. However, had there been the intention of government to give a gift of the right to vote, Bloomberg would have been a hero and called a Good Samaritan.

Race and Slavery in the Contemporary World: America 2020

Regime Elevation through Authority

The regime participants have built a position of authority in a manner to elevate their titles and anything associated with themselves, in value, esteem, status, reverence, and deference: Senator, President, judge, and the like. They resonate. The regime grooms us and requires us to obey without questioning any of their conduct or emanating acts unless they have given us the right to question them. In the Emancipation laws, they have given themselves the right to unlimited financial resources from every individual and granted themselves the right to have any amount of money irrespective of an individual's hardships, an individual's dreams, an individual's plans, and an individual's wishes or wants.

In addition, they allow themselves the right to sabotage an individual's reputation or sabotage an individual's ability to generate the very income over which they, in effect, claim ownership. In other words, not only does the regime impose slavery of punishment, the regime brazenly took ownership of all monies to be earned by the freed slave. This is evidenced in the Emancipation-era Amendment XIV. Fourteen states that when the regime decides its own financial need, their decision, and I quote, "shall not be questioned" by any individual the regime requires to financially pay for that which cannot be questioned. This means that the regime specifically declared that the freed Black man would not be the final decision maker in respect to his future financial holdings or earnings. This statement also means the political regime would be able to sabotage the Black man's work, destroy the Black man's credibility to block his income, while the regime participants have guaranteed income for themselves. Not only have they guaranteed income for themselves with their Emancipation laws, they created the obligation for the freed Black man to surrender any amount of money they decided he should surrender. In effect, this example shows that the regime elevated its own acts to a sacred level where they would be deemed unquestionable and secured their own financial income irrespective of the state of affairs of individuals.

As I mentioned, the strategic ideas of the regime, including what I have just pointed out, are put into the form of laws and if disobeyed constitute a crime for which the perpetrator will be punished. Since punishment is an obligation to obey the authority and obligation means owing something, the freed Black owed obedience to whatever emanates from the political regime. This means that Blacks freed from slavery would enter an America where those he employs, using the process of elections or nominations, charge him, the employer, whatever they feel like charging, him, the employer. Then the elected employees, who are participants of the regime, punish the freed Black (the employer) if he cannot find the money to cover the escapades of the said political regime (the employee). In other words, from a political thinking process, the Emancipation era laws were used to help ensure the authoritative elevation of the political regime above the freed Black man, in perpetuity. The political regime concretized the obligation of obedience to themselves and indebted the Black man to the regime. Did they ever intend to be considered employees of Blacks?

The obligations emanating from the political regime participants became more important and more valuable than us, our lives, our rights, or rights emanating from us. Legacies that generate fame and wealth for the roofs over their heads would become more important than the roof over our heads. Their funerals would be more important than ours.

When observing the Emancipation laws, it is clear that the political regime would do as they wish, or as they deem necessary for their ideas, wishes, and themselves.

Active Devaluation of Individuals

Not only did the political regime participants seek to set the foundation to exploit their Emancipation laws for material profit and the elevation of their authority, they also laid a foundation to devalue us with the notion of crime itself. However, I cannot repeat enough times that since 1789, whatever emanates from the political regime did not stop at these junctures. They created a climate to strategically elevate themselves, all acts, and all ideas associated with themselves, including laws emanating from their three branches, to unimaginable heights. They finally and brazenly placed all things associated with themselves above the Law with a capital L. I mean that they placed themselves and everything associated with themselves above the highest law, the 1789 Constitution. Therefore, the political regime was elevated above all laws. However, since 1789, whatever emanates from the political regime must obey the spirit of the 1789 Constitution. No branch of government and no act of any branch of government is above the Law, with a capital L.

Race and Slavery in the Contemporary World: America 2020

Alexis de Tocqueville and The American Vote

To shed deeper light on the landscape present prior to the Emancipation laws (1865-1870), allow me to tell you a little about Alexis de Tocqueville (1805-1859).

Tocqueville was a French politician and a political historical philosopher. Tocqueville spent time in North America from 1831 to 1832. He was astonished to find that there were people somewhere in the world actually living with such individual rights and liberties that he witnessed in the United States. Tocqueville interpreted his observation of the one of a kind American life of rights and liberties, as being due to the fact that Americans, in all brevity, voted for their President and their lawmakers. In his book, *Democracy in America* (1835 and 1840), Tocqueville named this modern American form of government after the ancient Greek word, democracy, as found in Plato's book that posits the base for government, *Republic* (375 BC). The modern-Tocquevillian American type of government under the word democracy would spread to many countries across the globe. However, it was Alexis de Tocqueville who decided that the life of rights and liberties that Americans were living was due in part to this election process.

Tocqueville could only attach himself to rights being generated or originating from a group, as in "We the People," embodying the country and that among that group, the political regime would protect equality between the individuals. However, for the most part, Americans were living with faith and trust in the Almighty. So, Americans had the very courage the French lacked—to be able to venture into a life of rights and liberties that emanate from each individual rather than being fearful of trusting each other. Each American had taken a risk by presuming that each individual was honest. When the individual has a genuine relationship with the Almighty, he sees proof of an honest individual each time he looks in the mirror because he meets Honesty, in person. In effect, when one experiences honesty by looking in the mirror, one knows with absolute certainty that honest individuals exist. So, America was founded on the courage to risk trusting individuals and to presume that all individuals are honest, by default. There is no other country in the world that is founded on this belief or adheres to this principle. This belief allowed Americans to make individuals originators and givers of rights. Then the American individual surrendered only a part of his rights to the group, or to the country, that could be used under the Constitution, even as a representation of the symbolic, "We the People."

To expand this, the Declaration of Independence, expanding on what Jean-Jacques Rousseau had taught the world in the previous century, recognizes that governments get "their powers from the consent" of the many individuals. However, as I mentioned, there were some Americans who wanted to make sure that America would be founded on individual rights; individuals would be protected from abuse, and rights would not be usurped or stolen by the political regime. The American concern was not abuse of any form from other individuals who were all presumed innocent or honest. The founding American concern was abuse from leadership; it was mistrust of leadership, of archi. Yet, our leadership grooms us to focus on dishonesty and abuse from our fellow Americans (the Tocqueville or French approach that brought the 1804 dictatorship) instead of a focus on the dishonesty of leadership and our abuse by them. So, after the two-year negotiations with many of the political minds focused on the idea of a Republic, those who had been insisting on a system of government with a primary foundation of individual rights and liberties forced the creation of a Constitutional Social Contract founded on unalienable rights of the many individuals making up the one America. The founding system was what I might call a Constitutional Social Contract. This means that, although Tocqueville described what he saw, his analysis substituted a part of his own political view.

In respect to Blacks in America, Tocqueville is important because he pointed out that people actually lived a life of rights and liberties that was unknown elsewhere in the world but with hypocrisy in regard to Blacks. However, he also shared his views that the level of rights and freedoms he witnessed in America was, put in layman terms, too much for Blacks to handle. He did not believe that Blacks had the ability to assimilate to a life with the rights and liberties he witnessed that Whites were enjoying in America. At the time, his view was the widely held common belief that Blacks lacked the ability to assimilate into a social system organized around individual rights and liberties because enjoyment of rights and liberties required the ability for sufficient self-discipline to make the sacrifices necessary to become highly civilized individuals. This meant that we lacked the ability for complete self-discipline to survive in a society where negotiations and soft signals direct the atmosphere.

Although this view is false, even in 2020, I have seen in the media, in relation to a person with Black blood, that the self-discipline required to make all necessary sacrifices to become a beacon of civility can harm a Black person on the inside. In a way, this view aligns with the notion of Blacks being closer in their feelings to other animals than to Whites. This is false. Contrary to the beliefs of those such as Tocqueville, every Black man has the discipline and the ability to make the sacrifices necessary to be able to live the most structured civilized life. Blacks are not destroyed on the inside by self-discipline.

Over the years, a combination comprised of Tocqueville's fear and the creation of criminal laws combined with cruel and unusual punishment of us has changed our brand from incapable of assimilation to, "Some Blacks are bad or dangerous people for a society of rights and liberties." In addition, discipline or punishment with the aim of taming the freed Black man continues to generate benefits to the political regime that allows the regime to be elevated above the Constitution and all the founding principles or expectations in America.

FEROCIOUS DETERMINATION TO ENSLAVE US: Take our Rights

Our political regime participants have established the expectations for Blacks, and expect us to be obedient and remain where we are supposed to be while they build themselves into the all-powerful and almighty. The slavery in punishment to which they have subjected us, diminishes us while denigrating and weakening our males. At the same time, the regime builds an image that promotes its prestige, authority, wealth, success, and strength.

When our males succeed in life or show signs of strength, they are placed under investigation and surveillance. They are only allowed to survive if they allow themselves to be used as some sort of token to further the regime's agenda. Even their usefulness does not always guarantee their protection from destruction.

Obligations versus Rights

The opposite of an obligation (debt) is a right. In law, you have rights, or you have obligations. With a laser focus on the obligation (debt) to submit, the officers and agents of the political regime are focused on a slave master dynamic. They have given themselves the right to oppress and brutalize us, and we have been given the obligation to submit. Our relationship is that of slavery, but we are the employers who are paying their wages.

Attempts by Government to Deprive us of our Right to be Equal to Them

From the time of the Emancipation laws, our political regime has worked to deflect from our being equal to them and our being equal to whatever emanates from them, including their laws. Again, they, and whatever comes from them, are no longer above us since the 1789 founding Laws.

Slavery and Obedience

Slavery and Obedience

It is a fact that the political regime does not care if we live or die. Only our submission to obedience is relevant and each incidence of obedience to the regime's officers or agents contributes to the strength and authority of our regime. Submission to the wishes and ideas of the political regime is an identification mark of slavery.

The regime has taken the path of grooming us to define, measure, and check equality in terms of ourselves versus our brothers and sisters—the same equality the French have, rather than the equality from our Founding Fathers and the equality found in the spirit of our Constitution.

As we focus on being equal to our brothers rather than to the political regime, the political thinking moves in as the Good Samaritan or hero who plays referee while dividing us to benefit members of the political regime.

Eventually the court gave into the reigning thought among our leadership within the country relative to establishing the notion of equality between individuals rather than between individuals and the political regime when they decided in the case, Plessy v. Ferguson (1896), that "separate but equal" between Blacks and Whites was legal under the

Constitution. Laws representative of this "separate but equal" principle are known as Jim Crow laws.

This allowed political thinking to further expand its power beyond managing our public affairs and deeper into our business and private affairs using race as a screen. It also allowed the regime to falsely inculcate the notion that our Founding Father's equality was equality between individuals. However, once again the equality that the political regime was supposed to be establishing is equality between itself (leadership) and the individual because this was equality about which our Founding Fathers spoke: between them and the king.

The entire notion of "separate but equal" was disingenuous. The political regime had already sent the message to Whites regarding protection and had already blamed Blacks for stealing property rights from Whites without compensation. When we look at property transfer, it will be obvious that this was disingenuous. However, this idea has been helpful to the advancement of our political regime.

Here is a look at some situations representing our modern-day slave condition, and our government's totalitarian tendencies supported by their notion of punishment.

The first is the story of Francis McIntosh, which demonstrates that the regime only views us as elements to be used and dominated as slaves. It also demonstrates that the regime will do whatever is necessary to achieve its members' wishes, protect their interests, and reduce us to the expectations and place they have selected for us.

The second story, that of Emmet Till shows that, prior to our overt abuse by enforcement of the political regime's policy wishes and ideas, we endured lynching at the hands of our White brothers under the shadows of what would became Jim Crow laws via our political regimes cunning encouragement.

Other stories of note include that of Rodney King, George Floyd, Breonna Taylor, Deja Stallings, and me, Patricia Yunghanns. Overall, all the stories were only possible because the policy ideas and wishes of our government have been directed toward holding us as slaves whether dead or alive, through punishment, while expanding their authority to unprecedented and unlawful levels. Since the new slavery is punishment, that is enforcement of disobedience of a criminal law that was created by government, our entire condition is the creation of our government.

Whites are blamed for lynching. The McIntosh story says otherwise.

Police are blamed for police brutality, but government's punishment in slavery policy ideas say otherwise. In addition, forcing a human to do what he would otherwise not want to do is brutal and cruel unto itself. The job of the police is to force individuals to do what they would not wish to do. There can never be a punishment that is a good enforcement inflicted on a human being.

Both lynching and police brutality are products of the government's drive or will to extract our rights so that they are our masters and dominate every aspect of our existence. Our murders, mistreatment, abuse, and oppression are merely collateral damage in their drive to fulfill their will.

Francis McIntosh: Can McIntosh Own a Part of His Life?

In 1836, Francis McIntosh, a free Black man, became the first known recorded case of lynching in America. The McIntosh incident did not occur in the South. It occurred in St. Louis, Missouri, where at least one thousand people watched.

The police had asked McIntosh to help them arrest someone, but McIntosh refused the police's demand. He was arrested for influencing (as in "interfering") with the police attempts to make an arrest. Had McIntosh helped the police, the police would have been successful in apprehending the suspect they wanted to arrest. McIntosh refused to be arrested for interference and ended up stabbing one of the police officers to death and injuring another. He was jailed. Whites entered the jail, dragged him along the streets to a tree to which they tied him, and created a wood fire around him. The wood was set afire and McIntosh roasted to death. From the famous McIntosh grand jury case, the judge voiced that the McIntosh case represented the "atrocities" Blacks were committing against Whites across America and referred to Blacks as "deadly enemy" of Whites. This message was sent by the judge overseeing the grand jury, however, the judge is part of government. The judge is a member of the judicial branch or section of government. This demonstrates that some of our leadership's thoughts already contained a representation of their Blacks as "deadly enemy" of Whites propaganda.

Why should McIntosh be responsible for the police enforcing the political regime's laws or be responsible for enforcement forces of punishment doing their job? Why should McIntosh's plans and life be less important than the job of the police? Because this hierarchy is the idea from the political regime as covered in their laws.

Why should McIntosh who has his own problems; who has his own life to worry about; who is burdened with his own boss who feeds him by providing him with a salary for his labor; who is already sustaining and taking care of government by giving them money for their salaries and functions through excise taxes, poll taxes, and property taxes, from his labor and his dealings irrespective of his challenges, his plans and his goals, be responsible for government doing their job? No one helps McIntosh do his job. When a job is too much for McIntosh, he gets fired and left with no resources to feed himself.

If government wants to punish and police, they need to be able to plan to have the capabilities to do so before they take on the new task. Why should government take on new tasks and responsibilities when they are not capable of handling those responsibilities?

Why does the political regime think that McIntosh's life exists for government's interest and convenience, such that McIntosh should be helping in the enslavement of a fellow American, while helping government do a job government unlawfully created for themselves to do?

As Rousseau pointed out, a well-functioning government is not busy punishing (enforcing), and he was referring to traditional leadership, rather than the 1789 American type where government has been given very limited power.

Why should McIntosh pay their salaries for doing a job and do the job for them even when it is not convenient for, nor in the best interest of, McIntosh to do their job for them? If he refuses, he gets arrested and goes to jail. He not only loses his job, he loses the potential to generate future income to feed himself.

Why should McIntosh let government seize, occupy, and take over his private life and private time?

The deal was for government to manage and develop the very limited part of McIntosh's public affairs as allowed in the Constitution. McIntosh was not responsible under the Constitution (Law) to assist the government in expanding the government's powers. In addition, the expansion of government powers is illegal.

Again, if a society of slavery based on punishment appears to be too much work for government, why does government not turn its mind to managing an America on rights and liberties instead of enforcement of its political policies?

I reiterate, it does not make sense for government to be expanding its powers and therefore its functions unless government has figured out how they are going to take on those functions without harassing private individuals individuals that are making sacrifices every day to be able to pay the salaries of the political regime's participants and make it possible for them to live in the type of luxury and exclusivity that are inaccessible to most Americans.

Emmet Till

In the summer of 1955, Emmet Till was visiting family members in Mississippi from Chicago when, in the middle of the night, he was removed from inside the home where he stayed. He was beaten, mutilated, and shot, and his nude body thrown into the river. His White killers were found not guilty. Till's murder sparked a sense of defiance in the Black community. By December of that year, Rosa Parks was motivated to disobey the government and refused to surrender her bus seat to a White person.

The Till story demonstrates that the same value the political regime openly placed on Blacks, Whites also began to place on Blacks.

Rodney King

In 1991, Rodney King was chased for a traffic violation in Los Angeles, California. He disobeyed police signals to stop, as he was being chased. When police caught him, they beat the unarmed King viciously with batons, using what they called power strokes. To this day, I recall watching the Rodney King incident on TV, at my home in Florida; I remember the feeling that the country was burning from California to Florida.

From watching the video, I sensed a deep determination on the part of the government officers to dominate King, dead or alive. Rodney King was merely a continuation of our regime's drive to crack down in certain domains, maintain our enslavement, and increase its authority.

George Floyd

In the summer of 2020, and amid the Coronavirus pandemic, George Floyd was alleged to have used a fake twenty-dollar bill at a food store in Minneapolis, Minnesota. When police officers tried to arrest Floyd, it was reported that one of the officers spent over eight minutes kneeling directly on Floyd's neck. Floyd was overheard saying words to the effect of, "I can't breathe." Floyd died, and his story sparked outrage and riots.

Floyd's story highlights the fact the officers were focused on arresting Floyd and that apprehending Floyd was more important than Floyd's life. Since police is merely enforcing the wishes of the political regime's laws, Floyd's value is the value the political regime places in its variety of laws and decisions.

Breonna Taylor

By 2020, our Black women were being pursued by government forces openly, brutally, and viciously. In March 2020, government police forces wearing plain clothes entered Breonna Taylor's apartment regarding drug dealings and ended up shooting Taylor who would die of gun wounds.

The Taylor case demonstrates again that, in the end, whatever the government forces wanted was more important than Taylor's life. However, the end they sought was what the political regime had decided was the objective.

Deja Stallings

In September 2020, Deja Stallings was twentyfive years old and was nine months pregnant. In Kansas City, Missouri, the pregnant Black woman was forced to the ground, face down, and a White police officer pressed into her back with his knee. The officer was aware of Stallings's pregnancy; in fact, witnesses had asked him to stop because she was pregnant. The officer was determined to arrest Stallings because she was not submissive. The ninemonth pregnant Stallings was arrested and charged with interfering with the arrest.

Again, Stallings story demonstrates that the regime's forces or enforcers were determined to enforce ideas from the government whether a baby ended up dead or alive.

Patricia Yunghanns: Opportunity for Racial Division

Prima facie, the story of twenty-six-year-old Breonna Taylor might appear very different than my own. She lived in Louisville, Kentucky. I live in Florida. Not everyone knew Breonna's name before her death. I, Patricia Yunghanns, on the other hand, am a descendant—the great-granddaughter—of a man with a street carrying his name. As a result of

his legacy and the financial estate he left behind, I was privileged enough to have been able to attend private school at a time when few people were able to do so; live in a two story homestead on the family estate, and experience what it was like to have people appear honored to cook, clean, and do the shopping for your family because of your family's past contributions to society. So, I understand a bit about stability, protection, and preservation of society and not striving to upset the status quo because of what might be my own negative experience.

I broke through the wall for all Blacks in polo, a sport on horses, but at its crust. The polo community practices the highest level of human social civility, and I had to demonstrate the kind of discipline Tocqueville didn't believe that Blacks could portray.

Some people enjoy a level of financial resources that allows them never to work a day in their lives, should they choose not to. Among these individuals are: the rich; the rich and famous; the super rich; the super rich and famous; the wealthy; the wealthy and famous; the super wealthy; and the super wealthy and famous. And then there are the polorelated groups.

At the upper crust of this last group, individuals are bonded by a common interpretation of the word, *sacrifice.*

People marrying into the polo world can witness the culture firsthand. Meghan (Markle), Duchess of Sussex would have experienced the closed and insulated polo world while married into the British royal family. Princess Diana's mother left her husband and lost custody of Princess Diana and her siblings to have a life with a polo playing man, Peter Shand Kydd. The mother of Sarah (Ferguson), Duchess of York, left her aristocratic husband to spend her life with a polo playing man, Héctor Barrantes. Princess Diana had a six-year affair while married to Prince Charles with a polo playing man, James Hewitt. Two of America's wealthiest heiresses, Doris Duke and Barbara Hutton, married the same polo player, Porfirio Rubirosa Ariza (Rubirosa).

I have served on the Steering Committee for Florida Junior Polo. Because the polo community "allowed" me—a Black—on the inside, it is now under ferocious government occupation and intimidation because of it. My story is one of harassment of an entire community by a government that is unwilling to take into account the harm and damage they are inflicting on all Blacks and race relations. The government's aim is not eradication of racial issues; it is to maintain division between the races and increase the authority of the political regime along with anything emanating from or associated with the political regime.

The government has used their cruel and brutally savage abuse of me as a Black Women to send a message to the entire polo community: that Blacks will tarnish and destroy your neighborhood if you let them in. They send the message that the inferior Blacks cannot assimilate at the highest social level. They send a message that their occupation is to protect polo and the polo world from me, the Black.

I am Black, so I am a danger. My strong ties and leadership roles in the polo community and my high level of education do not matter.

I am a member of the board of directors for the Polo Training Foundation. Since 1967, when the foundation was established to act as the training and charitable arm of the United States Polo Association, it has focused primarily on training and developing young people.

I am married to a no-longer-practicing lawyer who spent forty years building a private company from scratch, until the company was worth over a billion dollars publicly. Prior to university, my husband

had graduated from an exclusive private boarding school. He is also a founder of the new world wine industry. He mounted Prince Charles (for horse) when Prince Charles played polo in Australia.
He is a former vice-president of the International Federation of Polo. As such, I have had the responsibility of receiving and entertaining in our homes at the most demanding levels. This required diplomacy at the highest and strictest social level.

Our son attended and graduated from the most difficult school to get accepted into, in the world. He is now attending one of the eight Ivy League universities up North, and his university is the number-one university in the world for what he is studying.

I am myself highly educated. I have attended one of the six most prestigious universities in the world—the same one attended by Jackie Kennedy. My stint in medical school brought an element to my existence that discourages me from taking life for granted: I found myself dissecting cadavers, alone, in the wee hours of the night, surrounded by tables adorned with occupied body zippered bags. This experience changed my outlook on life, and I later committed to charitable pursuits. I have served as a director on charity board of directors, including Friends of Abused Children.

But I am a danger.

It is my firm belief that if I were White, with the same background, it would be laughable to conceive that I could possibly be considered dangerous, but the government considers me dangerous and spends millions of dollars informing the world that I am.

I am Breonna Taylor.

The government is ferociously determined to have me meet their expectations for Blacks.

Because I am Black, the government spends millions to have me (and other Black women) openly followed all day, every day, even on Christmas Day. We are under every imaginable—and unimaginable—form of government surveillance. How does the government get these millions? The schoolteacher is forced to not treat herself to a new pair of shoes because she has to give her hard earned money to our government so that our government could use it to unlawfully oppress and brutalize me.

The government even sprays us with radiation, which is dangerous because there is no scientific way of determining how already mutated cells in an individual will react to radiation that might seem quite harmless otherwise. Is the government breaking the law in doing this? Yes. The government is breaking the Law of the Constitution. Does the government care whether its actions are lawful or unlawful? No.

I am subjected to government harassment of all types including the type that would offend any decent woman. As a minor example, they appear to take photographs of the shape and size of my most private female area whenever they wish. In this case, the broader issue is the fact that government occupies the life of a freed Black woman whenever it wishes, as it wishes.

My own situation has taught me that our government would take any opportunity to humiliate, denigrate, and keep a Black person "in their place." It has also shown me that our government does not want integration of Blacks and harmony between Whites and Blacks because they are working to have the polo community view me as the government has labeled us. My situation has also taught me that government has no compunction in occupying and taking ownership of the life of a freed Black woman whenever it wishes, as it wishes to extract any rights it can.

In effect, the government has taken the opportunity to use me. I am being used in order for government to gain praise for ensuring the polo community and my all White neighborhood (outside of undercover government forces) have protection by government of Whites from Blacks. I am also being used to ensure that Blacks and Whites are kept divided. In this case, I just happen to be the example, or opportunity, the government could find and use. In addition, they inform the polo community that I am the problem and the reason why they are forced to occupy the life and space of some of the most private individuals on the planet. Furthermore, all my close friends are mothers who are not only of impeccable character, they are simply devoted family individuals in a sort of contra-celebrity universe.

Now, why would the Whites in polo trust allowing another Black so tightly into the pack? Well, after the government has used me to actively destroy all the trust the polo community can truly place in Blacks and deepen the racial division between Whites and Blacks, what will come from their political thinking? One day, another opportunity will surely arise. Yes, some day, when the government's interest or convenience can be served (they can profit), the government will say to Blacks: "We must establish equality. We are going to give you the right to polo." Or they might take the reverse approach: "The polo community is racist, and we have decided to outlaw polo. There will be no more polo in this country." Irrespective of the position the government will take, it will be to serve the members or the participants of the regime. At the same time, since whatever action the government takes will be by force, the White polo community will silently blame and hate Blacks. For they will blame Blacks for the government's crackdown on them. So, the government will continue to win because Blacks and Whites would be further divided, and this division offers opportunities for the government to play the hero and elevate its authority.

So, by telling the polo community that the regime is suspicious of me, the government is using me to demonstrate to Whites that Blacks are suspicious characters, especially since I am their close experience of a Black person. In other words, the government is teaching Whites that Blacks should not be trusted. However, Whites can trust the government to protect them from Blacks, in this case, from me. These polo Whites will teach their children and grandchildren not to trust Blacks, and the political regime's agenda to keep Blacks and Whites divided can continue.

To be Overly Fair to Government

It is quite possible that the government believes that I have been engaged in criminal activities, that I am involved in criminal activity, or that I am a potential criminally engaging participant. It is even possible that the government fears my intellectual capacity. Do take a look at the depth in my book entitled, *A Brief History of Change*. However, the government cannot legally occupy the life of an individual. It cannot legally reduce the life span of an individual. It cannot legally sabotage and destroy an individual's psychological existence.

Race and Slavery in the Contemporary World: America 2020

Who is more Dangerous?

Is my government more dangerous, or is this Black woman more dangerous? I am not trying to murder individuals who disobey me or might disobey me. I am not trying to harm anyone. I am not oppressing anyone.

Harassment

I am not harassing anyone. Our government is harassing private individuals visiting private property. Government forces are permanently and consistently harassing and interfering with the peaceful existence of private individuals on private property. This is illegal at all times: when it is done as obvious government forces; when it is done using and exploiting the lives of regular citizens, and when it is done using individuals whose lives have become a part of government's bed of deceit, duplicity, appalling, despicable, sadistic training, and the most disgusting infested web of gangster tactics and fear mongering intimidation.

Crack Downs

Again and again, slavery in punishment is cruelty. Whatever laws the regime considers important at the moment, will be highlighted for enforcement. Our regime can force individuals to obey the crimes they create or do anything they wish in order to dominate.

One question is how far will the political regime go? If we follow the pattern of political thinking, they will go as far as they need to go in order to take our rights while protecting and increasing benefits for their members, such as privileges and legacies for both present and future.

Post Flare-ups of Oppressive Incidents

We actually feel the oppression under which we live after the Rodney King type incidents. We experience flashes of the moments we have been called *nigger*; that moment we were told, "nigger go home," or the feeling we experienced when that lady hugged her purse the instant that we sat next to her. During the flare-ups, we find ourselves feeling a sense of urgency to put a stop to our condition.

Impact on Black Women

We feel the stories of our men. We know the images of our men being hunted down like animals through the cotton fields. We know the beatings they received. We know their stories. We know their humiliation. We know our own humiliation. We know our own stories. As women, not only do we know the stories of our men, we live a life of fear for the sons we carried for nine months. As Black women, we are impacted by the state and condition of all Blacks. From among ourselves, the stronger the Black woman, the more likely she has heard these words from her husband: "Baby, you should have come to me. Honey, you know I have your back." Or some iteration thereof. However, before the words were finished, she had solved the problems and closed that chapter.

Why Have We Failed to Negotiate Our Freedom?

In my view, there are two reasons. The first is our grooming to hide the taking of our rights, and the second is political strategic warfare. For the political regime, both are merely cautionary measures to ensure their perpetual dominance and our Inferiority.

Our Grooming and Predatory Signs

Gifts of Frozen Ice Cream Flavors. We are groomed by political thinkers with mouthwatering enticing frozen ice cream flavors to which they ensure that we become attached. These are always ideological or appear as something free of charge.

However, unlike energy, wealth can be created, and wealth can be destroyed. Government does not create any wealth to give anything free. They are only able to create laws to take wealth away from those who sacrifice their life, marriage, health, and family creating wealth. They then redistribute this wealth or transfer it to you while taking credit during good times and passing blame to the creators of wealth during any form of financial crisis. In addition, since 1789, they are no longer the holder of a reservoir of rights to give away.

Love and Deference, Connection. We are groomed to love and revere our masters. So, our masters are those we love, trust, and hold in the highest esteem. We believe everything they say. We criticize nothing they do. Again, they make us feel connected to them, and they make us feel comfortable with them.

We attend their political events, we give them money to support their competition to win the job. (They make us feel comfortable.) They say the things we are anxious to hear. They show hate to the selected enemy. They tell us they will fight for us, and we passionately defend them and fight for them. We find ourselves hating anyone, even each other, if words are uttered that indicate that the other is not a supporter of our beloved and trusted masters who change their policy ideas into illegal laws that keep us enslaved.

Strategic Political Warfare: Rights Transfer

I would like you to think about the following scenario for a moment. Suppose you take your five-year-old son's favorite toy and give it to his three-year-old brother. Now, you already know that the five-year-old will be angry and will probably begin to feel some animosity toward his three-yearold brother unless you compensate the five-yearold in some way. If you do not compensate the loser of the favorite toy, every time he sees his little brother playing with his favorite toy, animosity will grow and grow toward his little brother.

Rights were an important element in early America. Property rights are considered by many as the reason policing was first created. In addition, the right to one's property was a sensitive issue in early America. By not compensating slave owners while continuing slavery through activities such as Leasing, the political regime created problems for Blacks whom Whites would consider being beneficiaries of their property. Many Whites would have mortgaged their homes, taken out loans, and the like to purchase slaves.

However, it was not and has never been Blacks who received the favorite toy. The favorite toy was given to the political regime, and the political regime still has it.

Again, Whites think their property rights, held legally in each slave, were handed to Blacks, handed to each freed slave. Slave ownership was a right gifted to individuals by the political regime prior to the 1789 Constitution. Blacks think they were handed the right of freedom by the political regime.

In reality, there was never a transfer of slavery rights from the White slave owners to the freed Black. There was a transfer in law of those rights. The transfer of slavery rights occurred between the Whites and the political regime where the political regime was the beneficiary (profited) from the transaction.

The political regime carries no blame for the ownership transfer and take full credit for freeing the slaves. Yet, the proof of ownership transfer to the political regime can be openly observed in Leasing where the government provided the southern plantations and northern states with prison labor after the Emancipation laws. In fact, if we consider Leasing, classical slavery of Blacks, that did not exist in the North under individual ownership, expanded geographically under government ownership through Leasing.

Lincoln's intention at time of Proclamation

This is also where the question posited in the introduction regarding Lincoln could be answered: Leasing is one element that proves that there was evidently never any intention by Lincoln or any other politician to give Blacks their freedom.

On Rights, Change, Slavery, and the Need to Usurp Individual Rights

Our political regime is predatory by its very nature. At every incident, our government strives to remove and reduce our rights. Just as a vampire needs human blood to live forever, government needs to get rights from individuals into their own hands in order for government and its members to last as our slave masters. Different members of the political regime have different preferences for the segment of the population they prefer to use for the extraction or sucking of rights. Overall, a new political majority imposes enforcement crackdowns to remove rights on fresh groups of individuals.

The Rights give oxygen to slavery. They give legitimacy. Over time, they allow the development and enhancement of deference toward the regime and its members. Just as a vampire has a drive beyond his control when he smells human blood, the political regime (government) has a will beyond its control when it spots an opportunity to take our rights. Our enslavement becomes collateral damage.

Our government changes all the battle lines
our Forefathers created between leadership and
individuals. For example, they created battle lines
between individuals, such as equality being judged
between individuals rather than between leadership
versus individuals. Another example, the regime
makes us suspicious of each other and groom us
to hold them in the highest esteem. Grooming
and actions like blaming allow for slavery to
endure without the threat of revolutions or major
mutational changes.

In other words, rights are what is originally owned
by us. Rights represent the element that must
be changed for slavery to continue, for slavery
to survive long term. Rights must change from
the original owner, meaning from individuals.
So, the only way to avoid slavery is to hold onto
our rights. However, the political regime needs
our rights to be our master. The political regime
smells the opportunities to take our rights, just as a
despicable stepfather senses opportunities at night
in a teenager's bedroom. The regime offers to help
us; they offer us frozen ice cream flavors; they offer
us free things, including rights. However, all kind
advice, all gifts and offers from any political regime
is done eyeing how to use us to get our rights. It is
always predatory: groom and enslavement.

CHANGE IN DIRECTION OF COMPASS WITH PROTECTION

The third notable change in the Emancipation-era laws was a brazen compass directional shift. The direction changed from individual rights and liberties toward an elevation of the political regime's authority while depressing the possibility that the freed Black could ever threaten the regime's authority.

Political Thinking

Since authority is the power to enforce obedience and authority is necessary for punishment to be accepted, punishment can also be described as the enforcement or execution of politically generated ideas from the regime that is expecting to tame the disobedient.

The notion of individual rights and liberties transforming into increased legitimized power for the regime is in line with political thinking because political thinking will spontaneously generate ideas for its own interests. So, as the regime participants legislated on the abolition of slavery, they were focused on enslaving the soon-to-be free Black man. The avenue selected to achieve this change has been enforcement of regime-created punishment.

Again, the common focus of all the Emancipation laws was an Enforcement section that represented a pattern within the three Emancipation laws. Each law finishes with the political regime participants reminding us that they are eager to witness enforcement of their policy ideas. Each Emancipation law's last section starts with the following: "Congress shall have power to enforce this article." Some might say that such words have been used in Constitution. However, it was used only once: in respect to the integrity of the territory that was being pried away from "London." The fact that it was used in each Emancipationera law indicates that enforcement of the policy ideas and wishes of the regime was of tremendous significance to the participants of the regime.

In effect, the legislative branch felt that forcing individuals to obey them and enforcement of their Emancipation of Slavery era ideas were so significant that they expanded their wings to give themselves the power to ensure enforcement or execution of these Emancipation-era laws. In other words, at the same time that the regime legislated on the abolition of slavery, the regime focused on ensuring the punishment of the emancipated Black man through enforcement.

Enforcement is focused, by its essence, on force and forcing, and it is an oppressive use of authority. Enforcement is the most visible identification marker of authoritarianism and oppression, such as despotism, tyranny, dictatorship, totalitarianism, and the like. From the moment slaves were emancipated, the regime has been particularly busy creating reasons for punishment of individuals with a focus on enforcing their creations rather than building templates for public lives based on individuals with rights and liberties.

Enforcement of Punishment: A Definition

Since the Emancipation laws transformed the material of our country's needle on the guiding compass to enforcement of punishment, let us look a little closer at enforcement. I would begin by saying the following: Enforcement is the policing aspect of the strategic ideas of the regime. In addition, there is no good form of policing because all forms will exert itself as brutish, barbaric, cruel, and savage in fulfilling the policy ideas of government during crack down episodes. In practice, enforcement is what you and I recognize as policing. With the new enforcement era or post Emancipation, the future of all Americans is now paved in security policing or oppression and authoritarianism. This is simply unlawful under the 1789 Constitution.

An analogy, of the enforcement route taken by the regime rather than a path to individual rights, might be a scenario where one has been given the job to build, develop, and manage a group home for scholarly monks and a group home for popular entertainers. The path set out or template will be different. Just as a scholarly monk's group home development and management will not lead to a community conducive to a popular entertainment lifestyle, enforcement-based development and management cannot lead to a land conducive to individual rights and liberties. Another analogy is how you would manage the life of a son you expect to remain dependent on you while continuing to live at home for the rest of his life, and another son you are raising to move away from home and live his own life. The son who will end up with freedom will likely be taught or advised on strategies regarding how to establish rules for his own life because you will not be able to be a productive fulltime nanny once he leaves home.

Enforcement Infrastructure for Punishment

Enforcement requires an infrastructure, arsenal, or operating apparatus to ensure execution, forced obedience, or forced submission to the strategic policy ideas of the regime. Although enforcement is actually execution of rules as laws, in respect to punishment, *to enforce* is *to police* and *enforcing* is *policing*.

Those who carry out any form of enforcement activities are called police. There are various degrees of enforcement or manners of forcing individuals into submission of obedience. However, from an infrastructure perspective, the enforcement or policing apparatus operates at different degrees:

Degree A.

These are the agents in uniform who are just regular people trying to serve their community by enforcing the political regime's strategic ideas. We call them officers. Once the landscape for slavery became punishment, these police forces had to be created. So the 1800s was the century for creating regular police forces. For example, New York City created its first police force in 1845; Chicago created its first policing in 1851; Philadelphia created its first police force in 1855, and so on.

Degree B.

Next, there is the military just trying to protect the country or territory in time of war. Since a political regime will do whatever is necessary to achieve what it wants, the military will always be used from time to time against individuals to enforce the wishes and ideas of the regime. However, when used against the population, the military is performing as an extension or part of security policing.

Degree C.

Then, there is a third type of police that operates under words such as investigation, security, or intelligence. These words constitute the security degree of policing or enforcement and are tied to the protection of the regime or the regime's interest to the detriment of individual rights and liberties and in violation of the original Constitution of 1789. At the security degree, the regime operates in a perpetual state of exceptional circumstances necessitating all unlawful acts or actions to complete its desired mission at the expense of an individual's life and wellbeing. Lawful rights and liberties of individuals are totally irrelevant because only acts and actions, convenient for at least one of the three branches of government, are relevant.

The police forces established during the 1800s were not enough to nurture and expand slavery based on punishment and enforcement of the punishment.

Laws alone were not producing enough crimes. So in 1908, a full fledge investigation office called Federal Bureau of Investigation (FBI) was created by the political regime. The government has continued to build, expand, and create its enforcement arsenal, especially its intelligence policing copied from a model created by the British from whom we became independent because of their brutish and cruel mistreatment of individuals.

At the moment, the political regime is building something called a National Security apparatus. This might end up as a supragodlike policing force. Either way, it will be for the interest and convenience of the regime and for the enslavement of us, oppression of us, and usurpation of individual rights.

Godlike Character of Political Regime

At the security degree of enforcement, the regime is no longer manager, leader, or even monarch. Security imports a godlike character to the regime, and the police are groomed into crusaders protecting the symbolic highest holiness (the regime), along with all things associated with it, directly or remotely.

The godliness character of a regime that has security policing associated to it, reminds me of an article I read about an African country. The article spoke of an Osu people who were former slaves, but whose masters were gods rather than men. The article seemed to suggest that others worried about associating with these slave descendants socially and about potential punishment from possibly angry godly masters who had owned them. In other words, the viciousness of the gods' enforcement of punishment or capacity for potential punishment was enough to intimidate others from associating with the former slaves. It carried the power to create division.

On the one hand, the security policemen, like all of the policing forces, want to serve their country.

On the other hand, the regime grooms them into believing that the country is the regime and that the individual humans, making up the country, are nuisances creating problems or potential problems for the country (the regime). However, the country is actually the individual humans making it possible for the participants of the regime to live in luxury and change all their policy ideas into crimes.

A political regime with unlimited financial resources and no means to control itself will, sooner or later, use its authority to exploit and dominate everyone and everything under its authority in order to serve itself. This means that, sooner or later, such a political regime will use all individuals and all things as security agents because security is the strongest elevation element of a regime. However, it is not possible to achieve a goal of security and achieve a goal of individual rights and liberties simultaneously. For they are complementary.

This means that the Slavery Emancipation era laws audaciously changed the projection of America toward securing and expanding the power of the regime and away from the American founding principle of a country to be managed and developed on rights and liberties for the individuals. In other words, how can the same compass point in both the direction of security policing and individual rights and liberties if security requires the oppression of individuals for the benefit of those who create the oppressive ideas transformed into enforceable elements? Again, it is not possible for a compass to point in both the direction of security policing and individual rights and liberties at the same time.

Portrayed another way, our foundation is partly contractual. A successful contract requires relationships in the absence of deceitful and duplicitous acts and conduct. Security policing is deceit and duplicity personified in the interest of the regime. In reality, the direction of the compass reflects the direction being taken. According to the Declaration of Independence, a country should have a "foundation on such principles and organizing its powers in such form, as to them shall seem most likely to" result in the underlying guiding principles. Taking these words from our Declaration of Independence into consideration, our political regime is not organizing our country in a manner that will result in a country built on America's founding principles.

Frozen Ice Cream Flavor Coatings

Imagine for a moment that you hired someone to be your employee and manage the public life of the members of your club, your family, and yourself when the group of you are at the club. That person creates rules to be followed for the club's good functioning. Imagine that the manager is allowed to make any rule he wishes, and you have agreed to provide him with unlimited financial resources even if it means your becoming homeless.

Now imagine Rosa who has a club like yours but gave her manager a set of rules that dictate what he is allowed to control and do. Our constitution is like the Rosa scenario where our rule or law makers cannot lawfully make the laws their policy ideas dictate, their hearts desire, or their jobs require. Our political regime participants are expected to know the limits of their power, just as Rosa's manager would also know the limits of his power. With Rosa's system, she created the boundaries that would eventually tame and discipline her manager.

There is a third case that is outside the realm of political thinking where Elizabeth hires a manager who informs her immediately that he is privileged to have been entrusted with the management of her club and accepts the duty of serving her and the club most humbly (this can be seen more closely during another discussion). On the other hand, if he thinks politically, your manager will eventually dominate your lives inside your own home, and you will find yourself accepting his authority for your own perceived protection. This is the entrenchment of political grooming: domination from public affairs to private (personal) affairs and private (personal) relationships. However, this would have required political thinking on the part of your manager, and he probably used frozen ice cream coatings.

Division through Enforcement

Enforcement of punishment is a substantial source of division when the authority is powerful, just like the African Osu story I mentioned earlier. All enforcement under a cruel or authoritarian master engenders division between the punished and the observers.

Believe me when I say that Whites are not our enemy. Entrenched political thinking needs division. If it were not Blacks and Whites against each other, the political thinking would have rich and poor feeling disgust or suspicion vis-a-vis each other.

While our frozen ice cream coating is in the flavors of equality and right to vote, Whites receive the same signals and feel those same messages, but they have an extra coating.

Whites also have a double layer of frozen ice cream coating made of protection of self and protection of property, most necessarily, from the freed Black man. This signal of protection was gifted in Amendment Fourteen of the Emancipation-era laws. The key grooming words give an individual "Protection of the laws." In other words, the political thinking planted the idea that laws exist to protect. The use of the word protection infuses the idea in the minds of our White brothers that risks with their Black brothers and sisters should not be taken. This is contrary to the risk-taking path in respect to individuals that is the hallmark of America's founding principles. It is because Americans selected to accept the risk of death with individual rights and liberties over the protection the French sought from their government in respect to their fellow Frenchmen that America was able to propel itself to great heights. Imagine a life policing each other or trying to ensure that the lives of your fellow men are being sufficiently policed. This is the life of the Frenchman, but the Frenchman is able to point out all the areas of protection that he has secured from his political regime.

So, while releasing Blacks during Emancipation, the regime used one of the laws to highlight that Whites could consider themselves protected from the newly released Blacks. Jim Crow laws of "separate but equal" reflect this frozen ice cream coating of protection.

This indicates that many of our White brothers and sisters would accept the coating and would be prepared one day to accept equality in slavery if they could feel protected. The hope of being protected by the political regime from Blacks is based on a belief that at the end of the day, a politically generated thought or idea is capable of caring about something other than its own interests or conveniences. Believe me when I say no Black person could ever be as dangerous and cruel as power with unlimited resources. Our White brothers must recall that the Emancipation laws made our owner-master the same as their manager but turned surreptitiously into their owner and master, too.

Described another way, the protection political signal sows the seed of suspicion and mistrust toward Blacks. The punishment political signal sows the seed of disgust toward Blacks by discrediting us as a population and divides us from our White brothers and sisters.

All the frozen ice cream flavor coatings require authoritarianism in the form of oppression while appearing as gifts. This means that Blacks and Whites are groomed to be comfortable with and even to demand tyranny, despotism, or other forms of authoritarianism under an appearance of equality, and Whites are groomed extra to feel protected and demand protection.

Again, Whites are simply not our enemy. They are our American brothers and sisters. Blacks are bound to Whites, and they are bound to us by hearts that still beat for rights and liberties of our founding spirit and our founding principle. However, as Confucius says, individuals will, at some point, spontaneously imitate the direction of their master.

A GOVERNMENT OUT OF CONTROL

Enforcement or being forced to obey leadership is highlighted in both domination and slavery. Once the Europeans began traveling the globe and discovering that there were different levels of authority operating on people around the world, philosophers realized that humans were actually born free of all forms of authority and had once lived free of all forms of authority. Yet, around the world, the explorers and adventures fed them stories of people living under the domination of what could be called, "leaders."

They also realized that a newly born baby, at the instance of birth in a European hospital, was born just as free as a baby born in the jungle eons ago. The new-born infant was not subject to the domination of any leader. Some began to ask how is it that the newly born baby, who is free at the exact instance of birth, is subjected to the will of leadership as an adult. In other words, the baby was free at birth but a slave, for example, by adulthood. This became a paradox. This paradox was best discussed by Jean-Jacques Rousseau.

Jean-Jacques Rousseau

Jean-Jacques Rousseau (1712-1778) was Suisse but of French origin, and lived mostly in Switzerland. He had been born a Calvinist Protestant but converted to Catholicism and back to Protestantism. For a short time, he was a law clerk, and for a short time, he was part of a seminary where he considered becoming a priest.

Rousseau as a Target of Government

Rousseau wrote *The Social Contract* in 1762, along with another book. Both books were denounced by the Swiss government and a warrant was issued for his arrest. Rousseau selected a life as a fugitive rather than submit to government oppression. During his time as a fugitive, he used alias names. Again, for Rousseau, you cannot be both a man and a slave. The philosopher David Hume gave Rousseau credit for not fearing government and for not putting a veil over his true thoughts.

Rousseau's Description of the Slavery Paradox

Rousseau described the paradox in the form of a puzzle. From his book, *The Social Contract*, we find the words, "Man is born free and everywhere he is in chains."

For Rousseau, although each human is born free, how is it that in every corner of the globe, all humans are tied up in some degree of authoritarian chain. In other words, Rousseau stated that all humans around the world were now slaves to some form of human authority, as leadership.

Rousseau was also perplexed by this puzzle: if a man is born free, how can that man born as the son of a slave, be born a slave and not a man? For Rousseau, being human had the requirement of being a nonslave. Rousseau insisted that being a human and being a slave were opposites. For Rousseau, they "contradicted" each other.

Again, Rousseau was haunted by the dilemma where a human is born free and ends up subjected to a government, meaning under the authority of a leadership. He did not trust government bureaucracy, and he despised all government created bureaucracy.

For Rousseau, freedom with risks and accompanied by danger was better than a peaceful life as a slave. This is revealed in his famous words, "I prefer liberty with danger than peace with slavery." This means that Rousseau believed that one should always select a path with risks and danger over protection by a regime. He believed firmly that each individual had a right to risk his own life. If an individual refuses to take the risks, he surrenders what makes him human.

In sum, Rousseau believed that humans were born free with all imaginable and unimaginable liberties. He believed that a human is his own master. In law, this means that each individual is the legal owner of himself.

Rousseau also clarified that when he speaks of freedom, he does not refer to man being savagely out of control doing "whatever he wills." Instead, he is speaking specifically and precisely about a human

being "forced to do what is against his will, by any human power [human authority]."

Definition of Slavery on Rousseau's Views

For Rousseau, slavery is limited to the individual and he who has power over that individual. Again, according to Rousseau, a human "should not be forced to do what is against his will, by any human power [authority]." Rousseau's slavery pertains to government versus individuals. It is in regard to individual versus leadership. This can be government in the most primitive form to government in the most advanced form. For Rousseau, when that power forces an individual to do something the individual would not have ordinarily selected to do, the individual is in a state of slavery. From Rousseau's definition, all forms of government enforcement is slavery. In other words, all policing is enslavement by definition.

Analogy of Rousseau's Idea: An Agreement

Think about renting an apartment. The lease for an apartment that you sign is a contract; you will receive the apartment, and you will give the owner rent money. If you and the owner wish, you can go to the courts and have a judge change your contract into a court order. This will have the same enforcement consequence as any court order. This happened with the Constitution. There was a Rousseauian deal (contract) made between our Founding Forefathers and those who wanted to be our rulers. Congress's approval of the deal changed the name of the deal to Constitution. However, all the elements, making up the deal, are Laws. The Bill of Rights is a part of the deal.

As I mentioned, you and the owners of the apartment can go to the courts and have the court approve your lease agreement. If the court approves it, it becomes known as a court order rather than a lease and will have all the consequences of a court order. Enforcement of the lease will become an issue in the hands of government, the judicial branch (courts).

The Social Contract: Rousseau's Solution and Active Agreement

Rousseau proposed a solution to the dilemma, of a human born but only found in chains, in his book, *The Social Contract*. The conditions for Rousseau's solutions are that man is born free and without any obligation or debt owing to any entity; man owes no one anything at the moment of his birth; he does not owe obedience to any entity.

Then Rousseau added that man can establish a debt or obligations by agreeing to surrender his rights, his "person," to be changed into power for the purpose of managing grouplike public affairs. In effect, Rousseau takes the position that a human can select to be a slave if he gives his consent. A human can consent to surrendering "his person" to the overall "general will."

Yet, Rousseau urged that people should never promise to just obey authority. For Rousseau, if a people were to give a blind promise to obey authority, this promise removes the very character that made humans, humans. He believed that after consenting, one should participate in the management.

There are those who fear that Rousseau's ideas are dangerous because they send a message that when the people are unhappy, they can end the agreement, even by way of revolution.

Rousseau's Ideas as Practiced in the Contemporary World: People Participation

Rousseau's ideas form the base of governments today. Rousseau envisioned traditional sovereignty with the participation of the people where the interests and convenience of the common group trumps individual convenience and interests. Today, Rousseau's idea of people participation is called democracy.

America accepted Rousseau's idea that the focus should be people versus leadership. America also accepted Rousseau's idea that people should be equal to leadership. Equality would be in respect to individuals being made equal to leadership.

However, the United States made changes to Rousseau's ideas.

The American Way: The most surprising Historical Change

During the American Revolution, America began to forge and restore the natural state of freedom of the human being and create a lawful way to surrender only some rights for the management of public affairs. Americans began to consider the contentment of the individual and no longer the contentment and interest of the king or political regime.

The U.S. rejected the notion of traditional leadership that Rousseau accepted as, just the way it is. In the most spectacular change that has ever been known in government and one that most scholars refuse to recognize, America designated individuals, rather than people as a group, as the originators and owners of all rights. It limited the amount of rights that could be transferred to public management (government), and it limited the power that could be held under public management.

The United States was always destined to adapt Rousseau's solution because a White Southern slave master was never going to accept a path where he could potentially become a slave.

Although America was created to operate, be managed, and nurtured into a completely different and opposite country from all other countries in the world, America looks and operates like all other democracies.

Rousseau Requirement of Legitimacy for Slavery

Rousseau believed that when leadership has the power to force a human, this leadership needs to ensure that individuals see that power as a right belonging to leadership in order that people would respect it and revere it. In Rousseau's own words, "The strongest is never strong enough to be always the master, unless he transforms that strength into right." So, domination must be changed into a right. If that domination is to continue, it must be legitimized.

Law: Law is a tool that changes domination into a right. The greater the legitimacy or authority given by the law, the more deference and reverence to be received, and the stronger a legacy of leadership can be built and sustained. With deference and reverence, the political regime can avoid changes on the level of revolutions, in the event enforcement breaks down, by grooming slaves.

Money: However, I would also add that Rousseau's idea of legitimacy of power also requires financial resources in the form of money in order to ensure that a master remains a master.

So modern leadership has authority from law, and maintenance of this authority is based on the amount of financial resources (money) available to sustain it. Legitimacy changes power into authority and authority can be changed or elevated into levels of deference, reverence, and the creation of legacies. This is seen when looking at government changing its policy wishes into the creation of crimes.

Our American Senator: Member of the Political Regime

Several years ago, I saw a recording of a certain senator saying that unlawful actions by government are in a sacred category. He did not use the word, "sacred," but I understood it that way. I wrote down what the senator said, but I am passing it on to you without looking at my notes. So I am merely giving the gist of what he said: "How dare you compare the actions of government with those of the mafia? When the mafia commits its actions, they are illegal actions from a disreputable mafia. When the government commits the same actions, they are doing it for this country." How can doing something for the country be above doing something for an individual who makes the country (outside of war)? Even in time of war, the Constitution has placed restrictions on our government's actions.

Senators need to know the Constitution.

I use this senator to highlight the broader problem. The senator was totally divorced from the fact that he and other members of the political regime were not exempt from obeying the Constitution because their motivation was the symbol, the country. The senator's words relayed the message that he was completely divorced from the fact that a constitution exists and has laws he and the rest of his political regime must learn and follow before they make laws or engage in illegal activities. He seemed just as divorced from the restrictions placed on him and the rest of the regime as a two-yearold is divorced from the laws the senator and his regime colleagues were making that will affect what this eventual grown up toddler will be able to do and will not be able to do. By the way, over the years, I had heard the same senator make similar statements to the one I have mentioned but without the word mafia.

Senators need to Change their Out-of-Control Attitude.

From Rousseau's manner of thinking, the Senator's attitude was the following: "I will respect the constitution so long as I am pleased, and you will obey and respect my laws so long as I wish through my policy ideas."

The Senator's attitude was simply out of control. What do I mean by out of control? I mean rogueness in respect to the Constitution. It is analogous to total disregard and disobedience for the laws established in the Constitution that the regime must obey, and for the laws his own political regime was creating. Our government is out of control. I tell you: Our government is totally out of control. It does not respect and does not obey the Constitution that exists to constrain it. It acts as if the Constitution were a living document that is subject to their whims. The equivalent would be your driving without a driver's license because you had just arrived from overseas to take care of your dying mother, and this real-life tragedy makes it appropriate to drive without a license. Is this somehow related to the rule that without a license you cannot drive on a public road? In effect, the rule from government stipulates that without a license, you cannot drive on a public road. This is the rule from our government, and it must be followed. Irrespective of circumstances, the government will not change the rule.

In other words, the senator can instill his emotional word called "patriotism." I am very much a patriot and patriotism is critically necessary during times of war. However, the emotional patriotism is not the deal agreed to in forming the Constitution.

The senator had been hired to respect and promote the emotional tone or spirit of the Constitution. That spirit is individual rights and liberties at the expense of patriotism and any other frozen ice cream flavor any politician can invent. Instead, the senator openly pushed for acceptance of oppression of individual rights and liberties if it promotes patriotism.

Remember, patriotism is about the word, "country." Country can mean several different things. By pushing for brutality, cruelty, and savageness, it eliminated the definition based on individuals. You cannot promote brutalizing individuals on the one hand while promoting the love of individuals on the other. I inferred that the senator was referring to the political regime (of which he spoke as a member) and all things emanating from or associated with the regime, such as its laws when he used the word, "country." Remember a senator thinks politically and is a member of the regime.

Beware of Senators and their Frozen Ice Cream Flavor.

The senator was planting the frozen ice cream flavor of the emotional word, "patriotism" into the hearts and minds of Americans. Looking back at the sum of his words and the mafia remark that I had heard over the years, the senator openly presented the position that torture, murder, brutality, (all forms of sadism) and the like against individuals were acceptable if done in the name of country (patriotism).

However, country refers to territory, regime, or the individuals. Which one could this senator have had in his mind? Which one was he directing us to become fanatics of?

At the leadership level, no political thought can muster enough energy to be completed unless it can spot an opportunity for personal gain or some form of profit. The energy will not be available for completion. So, did this senator have political ambitions to become president?

Constitutional Crimes versus Legislative Crimes

The political regime's laws place restrictions on us and our property. However, our Forefathers' deal with them places immeasurable restrictions on them in order that they are allowed the power

(Rights) to make laws. We can drive a car but only if we have a driver's license. Our government can make laws but only if they and their laws follow the rules in the Constitution and the spirit of the Constitution. When we drive without a license, it is illegal, unlawful. When government makes a law that does not obey the Constitution, it is illegal, unlawful. However, our political regime (government) has placed other words in our minds to represent their unlawfulness, such as unconstitutional, nonconforming, and the like. Their unlawfulness, in breaking the Law originally set up by our Founding Fathers for them to obey, is no different than any one of us breaking any of their inferior (inferior to laws in the Constitution) laws. For the ideas and wishes of our political regime making up their laws to force upon us are not godlier than those imposed by our Founding Fathers upon our government.

You cannot drive on a public road legally (lawfully). So, without obeying the constitution, no law can be lawful, no actions of the government can be lawful. The senator who compared government behavior to the mafia obviously knew this, and yet he pushed for acceptance of the political regime's unlawfulness over accepting constraints placed upon him, on the basis of patriotism. It is obvious to a blind man that the examples I presented are unlawful.

As it stands, our government creates procedures it wishes to appear to follow. If it follows those and its forces follow those, the government considers itself as acting lawfully. However, our Founding Fathers created extra Laws that government must follow; laws that government must obey. Yet government breaks these Laws and most often, government and its members appear to not realize that these Laws exist. For example, they all appear oblivious to the very existence of Amendment IX.

Controls Imposed on Government by our Forefathers 1789

I continue to reiterate that a plethora of control mechanisms had been envisioned and put in place to ensure that each of us would be the holder of rights, giver of rights, and equal to any form of leadership and superior to those managing our public affairs. Individuals were declared the originators of all rights. The powers of government were limited to unprecedented levels that the world had never witnessed. A system of checks and balances was introduced. The principle of separation of powers of government was put in place. A Bill of Rights in respect to individuals was created. Finally, the press, that philosophers and thinkers had used for centuries as an avenue for freedom of speech and a platform where individual grievances regarding government could be voiced, was given a privileged place within the Bill for individual rights. Throughout history, philosophers resorted to creating their own newspapers or pamphlets as a last resort to government oppression. Let us think of Thomas Paine.

From the Senator's attitude, there is a sense that all precautions have failed. Actually, all control mechanisms have failed. Our government as slave master reigns every form of terror, harassment, and oppression imaginable and unimaginable.

Here are some concrete examples that demonstrate that all Controls have failed, and our government is completely out of control.

Principle Creator and Efficient Perpetrator of Real-life Crimes: Entrapment

Sometimes the government wants a person who has not committed one of its created crimes, to commit a crime so that the government could apply cruelty, savageness, and brutality to the individual. In other words, the government sometimes seeks a legitimate path to abuse an individual after having targeted or decided that they will abuse the specific individual.

The government creates or causes the creation of actual real-life crimes using officers, agents, or fellow Americans. They make sure that their target is a participant in the created scenario. Then they share their fabricated evidence with their other branches of government and succeed in destroying the targeted person's life. This is called entrapment. I cannot tell you how many times I have been put in a situation where others have tried to induce me to commit a crime.

Separation of mother and son

I was separated from my son at the airport while returning my son back to boarding school. The airline used the lie (pretext) that I had cancelled my flight. In reality, it was the airline acting under the unlawful control of our very own government that was forced to adopt the despicable deceitful actions of our government-security policing that refused to allow me to board that plane with my son and take him back to school. I cannot begin to share with you the harm and pain this caused my family. Can you imagine, our government has taken control over our private airlines and our government decides who can travel, when an individual can travel, and if a private individual can actually travel? Why would we give our right to moving about to anyone other than our parents? Our government does not have the lawful right to remove our right to movement. We never surrendered this to them. And why would or should we? Imagine: from being reduced in 1789 to the least powerful leadership the world has ever known, our government has built itself into an unlawful force that believes it has the power to dictate our movement by whatever means necessary. How, in the name of the heavens can our government, with the most limited powers in the history of governments, dictate to us, owners and givers of rights since 1789, when and if we are free to move? Who are they to sequester our private companies, who are they to put our private companies under duress and coerce them to break the laws of our Constitution? The members are those whom we hire by voting and with whom we must share any money we have so that they can earn about $200,000.00 each year and live in comfort and luxury. I continue to reiterate that our government is subject to the 1789 Constitution. Our government cannot legally dictate our movements even if it does not serve the interest of their unlawfully expanded powers. These actions are unlawful, and there is no path to making them lawful, other than a new Constitution. Who are they to control us beyond what our revolutionary forefathers signed us up for, in 1789? Their political thoughts will direct them to have procedures in place and evidence to prove that they followed their self-created procedures, but our government does not have all this power the members are throwing around. It does not seem as if the participants associated with our governments unlawful actions and activities are aware that our government is totally out of control.

Occupation of the Press: Palm Beach Daily News

It is my belief and based on what I have witnessed that the *Palm Beach Daily News* has been under classical government occupation consisting of governmental forces and/or agents without Nazi type uniforms or the most conspicuous weapons on display.

The First Amendment implicitly recognizes the Press as already having freedom. In addition, the First Amendment explicitly prohibits government from abridging or curtailing this freedom. It states that the government "shall make no law…abridging the freedom…of the press." This explicitly prohibits government from abridging, curtailing, interfering with, influencing, and the like, the freedom of the press.

The First Amendment says no law can curtail or interfere with the freedom of the Press.

The 1789 Constitution is the highest Law in our land, and all laws must adhere to its written words and its founding spirit. So, there is no rule, no law, no decision, no agreement, and the like that can make lawful what the 1789 Constitution has made unlawful. The government's occupation of the *Palm Beach Daily News* is illegal, and there is no possible avenue to make it legal.

Formation of a Deeper Parallel State

The lack of all control mechanisms and the possession of unlimited financial resources have allowed government to use enforcement of its policy ideas and wishes in the form of security policing to establish what I would call an unlawful "deeper parallel state." This deeper parallel state can be detected when any or all of the branches of government view our country as the political regime (government) and not as the individuals. It is also detectable when government associated participants act in total disregard of the Constitution: placing government above the Laws of the Constitution. Since the security degree of policing has absolutely no regard for individuals or individual rights because their undivided focus is protection of the political regime; since the security degree of policing is deceit and duplicity, and since the security degree of policing is always involved with conduct that is identified as deep parallel state type conduct, the parallel state mindset operates as if individuals were nuances or potential nuances of the political regime. One group within the parallel state is in search of disparaging individuals as conspiracy theorists, radicals, and the like. The deeper parallel state is not mysterious, it is government and its operatives operating outside the constraints of the 1789 Constitution. It operates in broad daylight alongside a dwindling and collapsing constitutionally legal state and with an attitude of the senator.

An analogy: Imagine a Mayor in a town where gambling is illegal. Imagine that the Mayor's Mansion becomes a casino at night, everyone who is anyone goes. Imagine that the casino has bunnies and all the bells and whistles. Imagine that these evenings are hosted by the Mayor and patriotic cigars are served nightly. This is the situation of our deeper parallel state that is operating lawlessly in broad daylight from Capitol Hill in Washington D.C. to New York City, and all across this country.

CONCLUSION

In spite of all the changes the Emancipation of slavery era engendered, there is one element that has remained constant and invariant. This invariant element is the value that was placed on Blacks. We are still not valued at one hundred percent human, and not yet emancipated from slavery. Our condition is that of oppression where we are subject to obedient submission to a political regime that continues to become more and more tyrannical, despotic, and authoritarian.

At the moment, we are tokens, exploited, and used in order to create a tyrannical state where there is equality among slaves for the benefit of the regime's participants, and this is risible. Why should we accept and support equality in slavery? In effect, is it wiser to select equality in slavery or risk natural mathematical probabilities for individual rights and liberties? The curtain has been raised on what our elected and nominated employees have been unlawfully building up. Moreover, on the one hand, they have been securing their security, authority, legacy, prestige, and wealth. On the other hand, they have been ensuring that individuals are oppressed and brutalized psychologically, financially, socially, and any other manner that allows them to obtain whatever they wish for themselves and government.

CONCLUSION

We must help to construct and develop a path paved with America's Promise.

My hope is that we could be recognized, officially and officiously, as five-fifth fully human capable of all civilized reasoning, conduct, and self-discipline to make any necessary sacrifices defining the most civilized standards; that we could help to ensure the Great Promise of America where all humans are endowed with unalienable rights attached to their being human, and that our core values remain our founding American Revolution's compass in the direction of individual rights and liberties available for all humans, even immigrants.

Today in Contemporary America, we live under government induced slavery, just like all the other countries in the world. Can we hold onto any individual rights in our private lives and in our homes?

Race and Slavery in the Contemporary World: America 2020

Tyranny and Authoritarianism

Tyranny and Authoritarianism

On July 29, 1921, the political party named National Socialist German Workers' Party elected a new party leader. Then in the federal elections held in July 1932, the National Socialist German Workers' Party won the elections and held the most seats in Germany's parliament (Reichstag). Their party leader was appointed Chancellor of Germany, a position held now, in 2020, by Angela Merkel. This is an example of participation in government or democracy. The party is known widely today as the famous "Nazi Party" or the Nazis and their leader, beginning in 1921, was named Adolf Hitler. Unlike Tocqueville, Germany, and all the other countries of the world, America's founding principles are based on rights originating with the individual and not with the political regime, the people, the workers, the king, and the like. Furthermore, unlike all these countries, America rejected traditional leadership. By establishing that individuals in America would be the owner of their rights and government powers would be severely limited, the American Constitution makes America phenomenally distinct from all other countries on the planet.

Yet, in 2020, it is my belief, that our government is unlawfully engaged in every form of tyranny and oppression imaginable and unimaginable, including psychological tyranny, on private American individuals and our on private lives. Moreover, it is my belief that our political regime uses catastrophic events, such as 9/11 and the pandemic as opportunities to exploit these tragedies in order to accelerate the tyrannical and authoritarian goals of the regime and to teach us how to question and fear our freedoms in order to weaken our American love and craving of individual rights and liberties, while they groom us to love their frozen ice cream flavors.

It is my belief that our government is enforcing unlawful laws, including unlawful regulations from unlawful agencies that have been unlawfully instituted. It is also my belief that our government is destroying people's ability to earn a living and feed themselves and their families, even blocking intellectual work from women. It is my belief that our government is unlawfully waging propaganda wars against individuals, disparaging individuals, and unlawfully destroying people's credibility.

I also believe that our government is unlawfully diverting and using information entrusted to various government agencies for specific administrative purposes in order to unlawfully coerce and put individuals under duress so that they would serve as protective-security policing agents against their fellow American brothers and sisters. It is my belief that alternatively, our government uses the unlawfully diverted information (under the guise of information about individuals is public information) to put individuals under duress in order that they would participate in unlawful government created real life crimes and get another fellow American who trust them to become involved in these government created real life crimes (entrapment) designed to oppress, brutalize, and inflict cruel and unusual punishment on Americans. I believe our government actively and intentionally seeks to murder Americans they consider disobedient or potentially disobedient to their wishes as set out in the wants and wishes of their government policies. I believe that our government is using unlawful networks of policing (security) that has been both secretly and publicly built up and continues to be built up, in all areas of our lives and throughout our country.

I believe that our government is unlawfully occupying private American businesses and unlawfully occupying private American lives. These occupations are causing enormous financial, psychological, and other damage on people's lives and people's livelihood. Imagine a government terrorizing people who are at work to earn an income to share with government and provide for the participants, including providing them with monuments that costs millions of dollars. Who would not be psychologically terrorized by government forces infiltrating or occupying your work space and forcing you to work with or be associated with someone who has had security police training?

Donald Trump: Supposing we consider today in 2020, the White House is occupied by a man who is accelerating the rate and current magnitude at which the country has been traveling in the direction of policing security revealed as tyranny and authoritarianism.

The other participants of the regime are cognizant of the need to use frozen ice cream flavor coatings and an incremental political approach that moves slowly and surreptitiously along the authoritarian path and toward complete tyranny. To prevent the swiftness with which tyranny will be welcomed, accepted, entrenched to a point of no return, and all chances of real Emancipation for us in the future will have dissipated, Donald Trump must be voted out of office.

I shall rename a very few of what I believe are his unlawful transgressions. I believe that Donald Trump has no qualms in using the unlawful network of policing (security) that has been both secretly and publicly built up and continues to be built up, in all areas of our lives and in our country. I believe that Donald Trump has no compunction about enforcing unlawful laws including unlawful regulations from unlawful agencies that have been unlawfully instituted. I believe that Donald Trump has no compunction about destroying an individual's credibility or blocking an individual's ability to generate an income from her intellectual work. I believe that Donald Trump has no compunction about unlawfully occupying private American businesses or private American lives, or encouraging individual Americans to serve as protective-security policing agents against their fellow American brothers and sisters. I believe that Donald Trump has absolutely no compunction whatsoever about executing these and other unlawful barbaric government acts and activities.

A SUMMARY

In summary, while slavery is merely tyranny and authoritarianism with less cruelty, race and slavery are intrinsically and inextricably intertwined. America was founded on and created a Constitution to build the opposite of a slave society. Effectively, slavery is being dependent on others for your rights to survival and existence. Blacks are associated with the word.

The Emancipation of Slavery laws meant to abolish slavery and free Blacks from slavery were laws that merely transferred ownership of Blacks to the political regime. The fact that the government continued to lease Black prisoners to plantation owners to use as physical labor is ample proof that there was no abolition of slavery.

In effect, the new laws subjected Blacks to the whims, wishes, and ideas of policies in the form of crimes invented and enacted by the regime and imposed on the newly "emancipated" Blacks while building the financial wealth, prestige, deference, and reverence of the regime and its members. This continues today. In effect, underneath the regime's definition of the word "equal" lie slave masters; underneath equality lies slave masters; underneath their gift of voting lies a landscape of punishment, and underneath their meaning of "protection" lies barbaric enforcement (policing) based on their policy crackdowns.

Furthermore, the political regime laid the ground for every possible sort of division, particularly between the races. Essentially, on Blacks, they nurtured us to think of equality not in terms of our Founding agreement. The founding connotation of equality in America was that each individual is equal to the king or political regime and each individual became the originator of rights, just like the king had been. Instead, they nurture us to think of our American brothers and sisters as the reference point for judgment of equality, just as all governments around the world train their people.

On the minds of our White brothers and sisters, they laid the ground for being protected from Blacks, except the very crimes are legislated or created by the regime (as rules in the form of laws). The regime perpetually creates distrust and suspicion between individuals with the occupation and violation of private lives and entities while criminalizing interactions between private entities and individuals. In fact, the regime inspires individuals to hate each other by discrediting, disparaging, and denigrating anyone who might even potentially disobey them, Blacks in particular, by even imposing preventive measures.

Moreover, in their new Emancipation of slavery laws, the political regime completely sidelined the obligations imposed on the regime by the spirit or agreement under which our Founding Fathers surrendered some of our alienable rights via the Constitution. By 2020, the political regime has grown to categorically reject all restraints placed on them in exchange for their having the position of trust that they were given. Now, they create procedures. Then, they follow their self-created procedures when convenient and refer to their actions as lawful under their creations.

They even reject the most fundamental element of all: the recognition and respect of individual rights and liberties.

By 2020, they have reversed the founding mantra from what they are obligated to do for individuals' rights and liberties under the Constitution to what individuals will do to help them unlawfully usurp the rights of individuals, to help them unlawfully oppress individuals, and to help them elevate their own authority and expand their powers while discrediting and disparaging anyone who dares to have a thought that they are not promoting with their propaganda. They have turned themselves and anything associated with themselves into the actual country rather than the country being composed of the individuals. In a broad sense, they expect the restraints they place on us, lawfully and unlawfully, to be accepted by us without questions, but they refuse to accept the lawful restraints that were placed on them under the Constitution in exchange for their being allowed to manage our public affairs in any form or fashion. Our government is the only government in the world with the constitutional restrictions that have been placed on them.

However, in their drive or will to be masters or "archis," they create and use racial tensions to camouflage the fact that they are unlawfully stripping us of all our lawful rights. In spite of the fact that America is the only country in the world to be based on rights emanating from or coming from the individual, our political regime has unlawfully adopted and imitates the position of the other countries. In particular, our political regime promotes that our rights are being gifted by them to us, or depend on them. This makes us by definition their slaves void of bravery, and it makes our country a continuously developing contemporary slave plantation.

GLOSSARY

as of November, 2020

Acts versus behavior:

In a general sense acts represent all paperwork of the government. Behavior or conduct is the actions of government.

Amendment:

An amendment is a change.

Branch:

Each section of government or area of power is referred to as a branch of government: legislative, executive, and judicial.

Constitution: A Meaning

What do I mean by Constitution? A constitution makes up the highest laws in a country. The American Constitution is the collection of all the laws that were created by our Founding Fathers. It gives certain rights in the form of power to government, and it imposes certain obligations on government in respect to rights individuals that continue to be held by individuals or that have simply not been surrendered to government.

What does Government do?

In America, since 1789, government is hired to manage the public affairs of the individuals of or in America. Traditionally, governments use laws to manage public affairs. In America, the constitution has severely limited what government can do legally or lawfully.

Government versus Political Regime

Rather than use the word government, I have selected to use the words, "political regime." In this book, government and political regime mean the same thing. Both terms refer to federal, state, and local participants. Both terms include the legislative power or Congress; the executive power or the presidency, and the judicial power or the court system. The legislative power is ultimately responsible for making laws; the executive power is responsible for executing laws, and the judicial power is responsible for interpreting laws.

History: USA

Not taking 9/11 into account, there were two principle changing events in US history. The first was the War of Independence that was a revolution against the government. So this conflict is actually called the American Revolution (1765-1783). This revolution ended in America becoming a real country on its own because it had been considered a part of what is now the United Kingdom with its capitol in London. At the time of the revolution, the main government was in London and the main leader was a king known as the monarch. The second event was the Civil War (1861-1865). This conflict was mainly between the northern states and the southern states. This was an internal war that ended in the reconstruction laws that I refer to as emancipation of slavery laws or emancipation era laws.

History: International Event

On the global stage, there was a major social event that occurred and impacted changes throughout the entire world in respect to rights. It was the French Revolution. It started with anger against the king (monarch) but ended with Frenchmen against Frenchmen.

Laws:

Laws are rules that are presented in certain forms and have followed certain procedures. I include rules from all three branches of government although the names of rules emanating from the branches are referred to by different names. In addition, there is a hierarchy to laws, even from the same branch of government.

Unlawful versus Unconstitutional:

Many times, I speak of unlawful. Although it is difficult to associate Congress or the courts or the president with breaking the law, since the 1789 Constitution, government can break the law, just as we can break the laws created by government. When government breaks the law, it means that they have disobeyed the 1789 Constitution. Most often rather than accusing government of doing something illegal, it is said that something unconstitutional happened. By using the word unconstitutional instead of illegal or unlawful, the reputation of the government entity does not suffer the same impact as the reputation of an entity that breaks a law created by the government.

BILL OF RIGHTS

Amendment I
Congress shall make no law respecting an establishment of religion, or prohibiting the free exercise thereof; or abridging the freedom of speech, or of the press; or the right of the people peaceably to assemble, and to petition the Government for a redress of grievances.

Amendment II
A well regulated Militia, being necessary to the security of a free State, the right of the people to keep and bear Arms shall not be infringed.

Amendment III
No Soldier shall, in time of peace be quartered in any house, without the consent of the Owner, nor in time of war, but in a manner to be prescribed by law.

Amendment IV
The right of the people to be secure in their persons, houses, papers, and effects, against unreasonable searches and seizures, shall not be violated, and no Warrants shall issue, but upon probable cause, supported by Oath or affirmation, and particularly describing the place to be searched, and the persons or things to be seized.

Amendment V
No person shall be held to answer for a capital, or otherwise infamous crime, unless on a presentment or indictment of a Grand Jury, except in cases arising in the land or naval forces, or in the Militia, when in actual service in time of War or public danger; nor shall any person be subject for the same offence to be twice put in jeopardy of life or limb; nor shall be compelled in any criminal case to be a witness against himself, nor be deprived of life, liberty, or property, without due process of law; nor shall private property be taken for public use, without just compensation.

Amendment VI
In all criminal prosecutions, the accused shall enjoy the right to a speedy and public trial, by an impartial jury of the State and district wherein the crime shall have been committed, which district shall have been previously ascertained by law, and to be informed of the nature and cause of the accusation; to be confronted with the witnesses against him; to have compulsory process for obtaining witnesses in his favor, and to have the Assistance of Counsel for his defence.

Amendment VII
In Suits at common law, where the value in controversy shall exceed twenty dollars, the right of trial by jury shall be preserved, and no fact tried by a jury, shall be otherwise re-examined in any Court of the United States, than according to the rules of the common law.

Amendment VIII
Excessive bail shall not be required, nor excessive fines imposed, nor cruel and unusual punishments inflicted.

Amendment IX
The enumeration in the Constitution, of certain rights, shall not be construed to deny or disparage others retained by the people.

Amendment X
The powers not delegated to the United States by the Constitution, nor prohibited by it to the States, are reserved to the States respectively, or to the people.

About the Author

Patricia Yunghanns is a well-established American writer who regularly contributes to the YouTube news channel "Human Rights News by Patricia Yunghanns." She's also a fiction writer who writes on science and philosophy through the lens of metamorphic history. Her novels, A Brief History of Change and The Origin of Awareness, are true treasures.

Yunghanns holds a bachelor's degree in chemistry and a Magistère from the Sorbonne. She has helped US Military servicemen in times of emergencies under the American Red Cross. She also successfully worked on the original national AIDS research project. When she's not writing, Yunghanns is committed to charitable pursuits. She has served as a director on various charity boards, including Friends of Abused Children. Yunghanns is a member of the board of directors for the Polo Training Foundation. Since 1967, when the foundation was established to act as the training and charitable arm of the United States Polo Association, it has focused primarily on training and developing young people.

Other books by the Author

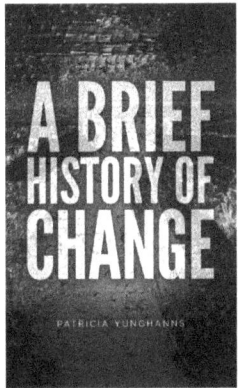

"Each day nature persists in its existence; it survives as flexible to present change and eventual changes."
-**Patricia Yughanns**

"Philosophical epistolary"
-**Kirkus Review**

Send the Author a Message

Please email the author any term you think
should be added to the adapted glossary.

EMAIL: patricia@patriciayunghanns.com
TWITTER: @yunghanns_

WEBSITE: www.patriciayunghannsauthor.com or
www.patriciayunghanns.com

CPSIA information can be obtained
at www.ICGtesting.com
Printed in the USA
BVHW070919220221
600771BV00004B/172